THE ROAD TO CLOSURE

A Journey Through Forgiveness

by

Karen & Ken Hartman

Bloomington, IN  Milton Keynes, UK

authorHOUSE®

AuthorHouse™
1663 Liberty Drive, Suite 200
Bloomington, IN 47403
www.authorhouse.com
Phone: 1-800-839-8640

AuthorHouse™ UK Ltd.
500 Avebury Boulevard
Central Milton Keynes, MK9 2BE
www.authorhouse.co.uk
Phone: 08001974150

This book is a work of non-fiction. Unless otherwise noted, the author and the publisher make no explicit guarantees as to the accuracy of the information contained in this book and in some cases, names of people and places have been altered to protect their privacy.

First published by AuthorHouse 10/4/2006

ISBN: 1-4259-5574-6 (sc)

Printed in the United States of America
Bloomington, Indiana

This book is printed on acid-free paper.

In Memory of Mary Monigold

A faithful woman who knew about hardship and forgiveness.

ACKNOWLEDGEMENTS

We have been blessed with an abundance of family and friends who help make our lives rich. We would like to thank a few of the people who have made this journey purposeful and rewarding.

Our friends Robert Butler and Pat Griffin encouraged us to take the steps toward making our idea a reality. Their support gave us the confidence to move forward with this project.

The time which Louise Taylor and Diane Funk gave to our project is greatly appreciated. Their combined editing efforts helped move our original manuscript toward the finished project.

Richard Arciniega's art work graces the cover of this book. We simply gave him a brief outline of our idea and he created a beautiful picture that we believe captures a moment in our lives, and the concept of our book.

Stan and Sandy Hartman have been a source of support without waiver. They were faithful in loving us when it wasn't easy or rewarding. We truly treasure our blessed relationship with them.

We praise God in our prayers and try to reflect our appreciation for His work in our lives daily. It seems appropriate to acknowledge God in print because it is His forgiveness that is the real motivation for this book.

TABLE OF CONTENTS

INTRODUCTION

Closure has become a popular catchword in the last decade. Its meaning is quickly understood as being associated with completion or the resolution of a situation. The word also carries with it a sense of peace, brought on by the reconciliation between people or even with one's self. Although closure is a state of mind, it can also be looked at as a desired destination. It is the ideal place to end up after we have weathered one of life's storms, because we know it is a place of rest.

The reason we hear the word closure so often and see the search for closure more prevalent in the lives of people today is because there is so much turmoil and discontent in the world. Our society is more crowded, complex and complicated than in past generations. As a result of living in a competitive and fast-paced world, in which the average family needs two incomes to survive, our relationships suffer, and, in turn, we suffer. The pain and resentment created and stored up between people can spill out and have a negative impact in every area of our lives.

Releasing, rather than storing up and holding on to resentments, is an essential factor in helping to stop or prevent unhealthy cycles from developing. Forgiveness is a key element in helping us to gain and maintain good emotional health. Forgiveness is a process that can help take us from the hardship of turmoil to closure.

We are going to look at the reasons why we hurt each other, what causes the pain, and how forgiveness can play a role in restoring balance and bringing about reconciliation. We will also watch the lives of several people unfold, and examine the losses and struggles they go through, getting a glimpse into how victims are created and failure is perpetuated. We will also see how awareness and desire for change can bring new hope and direction.

There are some unusual characters that we will meet along the way. There is a piece of us in each one of them, so it is hoped that you will be able to identify with their pain, burdens, and victories. In the end, a love story between two unlikely people emerges to demonstrate how the process of forgiveness takes one particular couple from total destruction to deliverance, and then into closure.

Closure is not something that happens by accident. We cannot depend on some event or somebody to take us to closure. Forgiveness allows us to be involved in the direction of our own lives. It is a journey with many potential twists and turns, and we need to be active participants if we want to arrive at the desired destination.

CHAPTER 1

WHERE DOES IT START, WHERE DOES IT END

{ Old Man Jake }

There used to be an old man named Jake, who would wander into a nearby town every spring. He had the sad and distinct look of a broken man as he walked the streets of a run-down neighborhood while going about his daily business. No one ever knew exactly what he was doing or even from where he had come. There were rumors he had passed through this town years ago as a young man, and had been returning regularly ever since.

The only thing more consistent than the old man's routine was his disgusting appearance and dreadful attitude. Jake didn't take good care of himself. He was unsightly and smelled of decay, always dressed in used-up clothing, and walking in shoes that had long since been worn through. He either didn't care about his own appearance or, possibly, didn't have the ability to change his unfortunate situation. His physical mannerisms and unkempt appearance added to the overall unpleasant experience people had when coming into contact with him.

"Grumpy old man" would have been a kind description of Jake. He wore a hardened face and had a glare that said beware to anyone who got close enough to feel its animosity. The negative energy that radiated from him was so intense that it could be felt in the stomachs and tasted in the mouths of those who passed too close.

As the years went by, Jake could be seen each spring living out what must have been a miserable existence. But in some strange way, Jake seemed to be content in his world. Perhaps he simply didn't know of any other manner in which to live, and had long ago gotten used to the pain that followed him everywhere he went.

Countless seasons passed and Jake's health began to fail. He had no obvious illness; nonetheless, his situation went from grim to grave. It probably couldn't be said that Jake enjoyed life or found much purpose in his aimless routine, and yet, he was oddly comfortable with the misery that dwelled within him and guided his path. Jake eventually deteriorated to the point of death. He died as he had lived, alone and out of touch, not only with himself, but with the rest of the world, as well. It is doubtful that he ever intended to live and die in such a hopeless state and unforgiving place, but that is how it played out.

There is no way of knowing where Jake started out in life or exactly when it was that life had dealt him enough blows to knock him off-track. Certain is the fact that he died in a town where he spent a great deal of time, a place called "Anger." It has been said that among his many travels and temporary dwelling places, Jake would usually spend the long, hot summers in the town of "Resentment." He was likely to be found in "Revenge" during the fall, and tradition holds that he spent his winters in "Isolation."

It does not seem logical that wandering from one painful and unproductive place to another could have been Jake's goal in life. Why would he remain caught up in this senseless pattern? Most rational people believe that his true destination and the place he really longed to live in was the peace-filled town of "Closure." But, for some reason, he could never find the right direction, and no one in the places he frequented was willing or able to guide him. In fact, the people in the towns where he stayed never wanted to see Jake leave, because as long as a pitiful old man like Jake was around, they didn't feel too bad about their own miserable and unfulfilled lives.

Somewhere in his past, others had hurt Jake, probably people whom he knew and cared about. Sadly, he was never able to overcome the pain he had absorbed. Who knows how many hardships he endured as he wandered from town to town in his self-imposed destructive cycle? Jake could never grasp the unchanging reality that the only way to get to the town of "Closure" is by first passing through "Forgiveness."

Jake's life is only one among countless others that has ended on some lonely road. Tragically, there are too many similar stories being played out right here and now. The poison that is spread through unforgiveness will cause the lives of too many people to end, without them ever having experienced the peace and freedom that can be found in a place called "Closure." It doesn't have to be that way.

{ The Endless Search For Balance }

If you look at how involved and complicated this world can be, it would be unreasonable to believe anyone could navigate his way through life without having to endure a variety of hardships. Considering all of the contact we have with countless people over a lifetime, how could there not be conflict within us and around us? Problems begin to arise as each person strives to fulfill his most basic needs, and that is just the beginning.

The human body is involved in a lifelong struggle to gain and maintain balance from the very moment of conception. The body fights a never-ending battle to bring its many systems together, working in harmony. This need for balance is found in every aspect of human function and behavior. From the operation of a single cell in your body to the most complex emotional needs, it is all about balance.

We are inherently equipped with an instinctive need and desire to provide for ourselves that which the body requires in order to maintain balance. Nutrition and shelter are on the top of the list of things we need to pursue daily. In fact, our lives are centered on obtaining these basic items. It may not appear that way in our modern society; we, as a civilized people, desperately want to believe there is so much more to us than such simple issues as food and shelter. However, the reality is that these fundamental needs have to be met in order for anything and everything else to happen in our lives.

It is during this search to sustain natural balance that we are introduced to some of the flaws in our human nature. Losing perspective and not being able to differentiate between need and greed is a common occurrence in man's search for balance. There can be a fear of not getting a proper share or not appearing to have succeeded at these endeavors, which breeds an unhealthy competitive spirit. If people can lose the proper perspective in the attempt to obtain the most basic of needs, it should not be surprising that as we seek to fulfill our deeper needs, there is a greater potential for disaster during the journey through life.

Interwoven with the basic needs are the deeper or emotional needs that everyone has. We are inwardly driven to supply our hearts and minds with all they require. The needs themselves are not the problem; it is normal and healthy to want love, to search for our identity, to find purpose, and to be accepted by others. Most people would like to belong, to feel as if they are a part of a greater whole, but we often spend too much time and energy shaping ourselves and making adjustments to fit a desired mold or to appear to be what we think others want us to be.

The question "what is my purpose in life?" is one of the oldest aspects of human consciousness. For us to discover our purpose and find an identity is extremely important, but in the pursuit of defining "self," the rights and needs of other people should not be violated. If someone creates for himself an image or a purpose, and becomes willing to uphold that image or fulfill that purpose at any cost, then people are going to be hurt, emotional damage will occur, and the victims are left to deal with the baggage that is likely to be created.

{ Is There Any Way To Find Balance In Love? }

What about love? Love is the best thing and the worst thing that ever happens to us. The definition of love is easy; love is confusing and complicated. You may try to give love and the object of your love will not receive it. You might enjoy expressing your love in words, but the effort goes unappreciated, because the person you are sharing your love with would much rather see your love expressed in a more practical or material form. Nothing else can span and stretch the spectrum of human emotions like love. It brings pleasure that will sometimes end quickly, followed by pain that just won't cease. What else can make you feel so secure and so vulnerable all at the same time? Love can help make you complete and give you purpose. It can make you feel alive, and then turn around and make you wish you were never born. Love can drive your desire to create new life, and it can push you to the point of taking a life. Love will have you wanting to give everything, and then leave you wondering why you did it. The need for love is the greatest cause of suffering and the single source for healing our suffering.

We create and endure more emotional pain in our pursuit of love than in any other area of our lives. Striking a balance in matters of the heart is a tough challenge, indeed. If we are to survive this challenge in a healthy way, we will have to be willing and able to give and receive forgiveness in order to restore balance and help meet the needs of those we love.

Remembering that it is more important to love people than to love things is one step in the right direction toward finding balance, and if we could just practice this truth, we would save ourselves countless hardships. Of equal value is the knowledge that there are many forces working against us as we endeavor to find balance in these areas. There are certain hindrances that have to be confronted and overcome. These roadblocks come from numerous sources and angles. We will be hindered by others, by life itself, and, most of all, by ourselves.

{ Roadblocks At Every Turn }

Why would we hinder ourselves during the search and pursuit of balance? It doesn't make sense to obstruct your own path. The saying about being your own worst enemy may be an old, worn-out expression, but it is absolutely true. We can create and perpetuate situations in which we are both the perpetrator and the victim. The damage that we have absorbed over the years influences our thoughts and actions. It can also have a negative effect on our lives presently, and in the future. In many cases, the source, which prevents us from fulfilling our needs, can be found by looking in the mirror.

Other people will hinder us as well; certainly, most of us have experienced this reality in our lifetimes. How and why people hinder us, and what can be done to minimize the occurrences and damage sustained in these conflicts will be explored briefly here, and to a greater degree later.

Much of what other people do is outside our circle of influence. While people attempt to secure their own needs, the character defects that govern their lives can spill over and violate the rights and needs of others. This can happen quite by accident or out of ignorance, in some cases. In less innocent situations, we find those who purposefully obstruct the paths of others, spurred on by greed or any number of other selfish motives in their repertoire. Sometimes it may be as simple as different values or agendas that bring about conflict. Although the actions of others is out of our control, our reaction to every situation we encounter is very much within our control, and it is our responsibility to make healthy choices on our own behalf.

Life itself comes with a variety of pain and roadblocks that can slow or stop progress. From the weather, all the way to major economic changes in our free capitalist society, there are seemingly endless bombardments of potholes and detours that are dropped in our path.

The world we live in may be highly mechanized and technically advanced, but it is also emotionally immature and extremely selfish. Our natural drive and desire to get what we want has turned into an ugly competition where there are no rules. Many people are guided into destructive patterns of behavior by selfish motives, and "anything goes" has become the slogan of the day.

{ Baggage Slows You Down }

Being disappointed in people, in ourselves, and with life in general can easily lead to a person falling short of his personal and natural goals. The results of our efforts to exist and interact with the rest of the people on this planet can lead us to a point where we begin to develop our own less-than-healthy methods for dealing with life, and obtaining the things we need and desire.

Stored resentments can often be found at the root of our discontent. This single issue of not being able to let go of past and present harms that have been inflicted upon us can cause immeasurable damage and impact our lives in ways beyond comprehension. Without healthy methods for dealing with and releasing the pain we pick up along the road, there can be an accumulative effect that leaves us with unresolved conflict. These inner burdens will fester and eventually manifest themselves in ways that will take a toll on the physical, emotional, and spiritual health of us and the people we care about.

{ The Search For Relief }

Rather than being satisfied with just storing up life's burdens and settling for less than a peaceful and healthy life, why not search for resolution? It is in our nature to avoid and relinquish ourselves of all forms of pain. The list of avenues that we will go down to find relief from the barrage of burdens raining down on us is endless.

On one end of the scale of methods to find relief, we see people trying to get in touch with themselves, or maybe trying to get outside of themselves. Some try to lay hold of that which is good, and others concentrate on releasing that which is bad. There are teachings on how to find the child within, how to lock out evil, and how to welcome love in; the list goes on and on. Although going into any of these methods in greater detail is outside the scope of this book, it is appropriate to mention here that at the foundation of any system, or faith practice, must be the willingness to forgive others and forgive ourselves. Without this fundamental truth being realized and executed, there is no way of reaching our ultimate goals.

On the other end of the scale of methods used to seek relief from our unresolved issues, the search for resolution can take us down some less desirable and even dangerous roads. The world offers plenty of inappropriate ways of dealing with pain and the people or causes of that pain. The upside to these methods (if there is one) is that they can have quick results and can even be fun in their application (depending on how you define fun). The downside to any method that is about pleasure, revenge, or cover-up, instead of discovery and healing, is that the relief is bogus in nature and only temporary. In addition, further damage is likely to be incurred and there can be life-long consequences.

{ Current State Of Mind }

Life can often leave us in a state of dissatisfaction, with a sense of being penned-up, frustrated, and incomplete. What we desire is to have things in their proper order and perspective, but we settle for doing things the way we have always done them, because that is what we are familiar with and what is easiest. The sad reality of remaining in this traditional mindset is that we can unwittingly go quietly through life in a condition of discomfort, but oddly satisfied with less than we deserve.

{ New Direction }

The intent of this book is to hopefully lend some assistance and provide productive alternatives in the transition away from unhealthy traditions and ingrained methods of dealing with the burdens and resentments that tend to accumulate in our lives. Just as in the story of the old man named Jake, we all have an inward desire to move from a place of discomfort to closure. Closure is a place of rest and peace. It is a quiet, safe, and secure place, where there is no madness or hidden agendas. The only problem is getting there.

Before any journey or venture can be undertaken, there first must be a desired goal or destination, followed by a plan of execution, and a real commitment to the success of the journey. It is necessary to be aware of the potential setbacks and remain focused on the rewards that lay on the other side of the hardships that will be encountered along the way.

There are some unhealthy mindsets and traditions that we have been conditioned under that will have to be considered and addressed. You may have grown up in an environment that promoted prejudice or with a family that was unreasonably demanding and unforgiving. In any of these cases and in countless situations not mentioned here, the mind has been poisoned. Unfortunately, this is often a multi-generational cycle in which the poison is administered to us and in turn, we perpetuate the cycle by unknowingly passing it on to others. Sadly, it is the people we love onto whom we pass the poison.

The problem of being conditioned in ways that are not in our best interest reaches beyond the family. We live in a society that believes a person's success and value is directly linked to material possessions. The emphasis is on getting your share before someone else gets to it first. "Be all you can be," regardless of who gets hurt in the process. Bigger, better, and faster is what we have been conditioned to value. If someone hurts you, make him or her pay for it. If you hurt someone else, never admit you are wrong. This particular philosophy will take you to a lot of places, but it will never take you to a place called "Closure."

{ Who Can I Blame? }

Isn't it true that we have become a society of victims? Why own up to your responsibilities, why should you forgive someone and work through the pain you have absorbed, when all you have to do is join the "Poor Me Society." We seem to be encouraged from every angle to embrace being a victim, grow comfortable in the role, and use it for all it is worth.

Dr. Douglas K. Smith[1] wrote an article on the subject titled "Who is to Blame?" In his article, he uses an effective word picture to illustrate why we should keep the act of assessing blame in its proper perspective. The analogy he uses was one of firemen arriving at a burning house. The firemen concentrate their efforts on putting out the fire. Discovering the cause and source of the fire has its part in the overall process, but it certainly is not the primary objective. Finding out who started the fire will not fix the house. It seems that, all too often, we get stuck in blame and never move on to a better place.

{ It's All About You }

In order to effectively navigate through life and still maintain your health and proper value system, it is imperative to have a serious commitment to your own well-being and to gather the necessary skills to help ensure your success. One essential skill that is needed, and, in turn, will pay great dividends, is forgiveness. Forgiveness is not automatic; it can take some real work to accomplish. The act of forgiving is actually more about you than the person you are forgiving, because you are the one who receives the greatest reward: freedom from the burdens that come with unforgiveness. Forgiveness is a gift that you give to yourself, and only you can give it.

CHAPTER 2

A LOOK AT THE PROBLEM AND THE PAIN

{ A Walk With Annie }

Annie came out her front door early today. It rained last night, but it is a clear and cool morning. Closing the door behind her, she walks off the porch, down the stairs, and is on her way to the bus stop. Annie is glad to be getting out of the house and heads off to her fifth grade classroom. Things aren't really good at home for her right now, so the school day offers a welcome distraction from her domestic situation.

Heading down the sidewalk, she passes her neighbor, Mrs. Norris, bringing the garbage out of her house. Mrs. Norris doesn't notice Annie walking by this morning; she is preoccupied with her own personal concerns. Mrs. Norris has custody of her grandson, Brandon. Her daughter is a single mother, who can't quite keep it together well enough to care of herself, so she certainly can't properly provide for her teenage son. Mrs. Norris took over the care of Brandon about a year ago, and has been raising the young man ever since.

Last night, Brandon went out with some friends and hasn't come home yet. Mrs. Norris is taking her trash out with a heavy heart this morning. She is concerned and angry at the same time. She loves Brandon and cannot understand why he would stay out and not call. He should know she has been up all night worrying.

Annie crosses the street and walks toward the corner, where she sees Bobby Roberts out in front of his house, washing his car. Annie has known Bobby for most of her young life. He used to baby-sit her a few years ago, when she was a toddler. She remembers that he was always nice to her and he continues to be friendly whenever their paths cross. Bobby has been away at college all year, but he has taken a couple of days off to come home for his sister's wedding this weekend. He is wrestling with some issues of his own this morning. Tomorrow will be the first time Bobby will meet his mother. She left when he was a baby and hasn't been around since. He heard she is in town and is expected to show up for the wedding. Bobby greets Annie with a glance and they both move past the moment and on with the rest of their day.

Annie arrives at her bus stop in time to visit with a few of her classmates. They are all huddling together at the corner, chatting, when a car races around the curve and comes dangerously close to the children. The tires run through the puddle that gathered after last night's rain, splashing cold, muddy water on the children. The kids are now drenched and not at all happy with the unknown driver.

A local man named Jack is the driver. He scarcely notices the children, and has no idea how he has disrupted their day. Jack is not focused this morning; he is still feeling the effects of having spent most of last night drinking at his favorite bar. He and his wife got into a fight yesterday, so he thought he would teach her a lesson by not coming home until the early hours of the morning. Now he is paying the price for his twisted logic. Jack is miserable today; he knows he is supposed to be mad at his wife, but he can't remember exactly what it is that they were fighting about.

Annie gets past the splashing incident and quietly goes on with her day. After a long and uneventful day at school, she finds herself back at the same bus stop, preparing to walk the few blocks that lay between it and her house. She stops along the way at the neighborhood market, which is owned and run by a retired couple. Annie has saved a little change throughout the week and decides to treat herself to a candy bar. The storeowner has never been a very friendly man, but today he seems to be in an exceptionally foul mood. Apparently, someone has been vandalizing the store, and the owner assumes it is some of the kids in the neighborhood. The man is aware that he is being less than friendly to the young girl, but he justifies his actions in his mind as fair and logical. He thinks to himself, "If these kids wouldn't tear up my property, then I wouldn't be so mean." As Annie is leaving the store, she thinks to herself, "If that man wasn't so mean, maybe people wouldn't keep vandalizing his store."

The last couple of blocks on the way home are long and lonely for Annie. In the back of her mind, Annie has known all day that this moment would come. There were a few points during the day when she almost forgot about the dreaded walk home. The fact that it is Friday doesn't help her anxiety. The problems at home can be compounded on Friday, because it is payday, and that brings a whole new set of problems into the house.

Annie finds some relief during the last few steps of today's journey, when she realizes she has one thing to be thankful for: at least no one noticed or asked about the bruises on her body today. That's one less thing to worry about. She must have done a good enough job dressing herself to cover up all of the marks, or maybe everyone along the way was just too busy with their own problems to notice.

Is there anyone in this short story with whom you can identify? Are you one of the people causing the pain, or one of the people in pain? (Perhaps you are both.)

{ All People Are Equal, In Some Ways }

Everyone is affected by the actions of others, and in turn, that which has affected us will in some way pass through us and move into the lives of others.

Life is fair to all people in at least one small respect. Everyone has an equal opportunity to experience firsthand the frustration of trying to maneuver through life without sustaining too much damage at the hands of others. There are potential hazards at every turn.

{ They Know, Or Do They? }

People can disrupt your life purely by accident, without ever having met you until the moment of impact. The impact could be in the form of someone walking out of a job interview with a position you were trying to get. The moment of impact could be as simple as bumping into another person in the grocery store, or, in a much more serious case, the actual impact of two cars colliding.

In some encounters with other residents of planet earth, it would appear that those who invade your space and infringe upon your rights are perfectly aware of the violation as it occurs. Unfortunately, people often act in a way that any thoughtful person would consider disrespectful. Probably the toughest situations to understand, endure, and try to work through, are when people with a blatant disregard for the rights, feelings, and possessions of others invade our world. The degree and level of severity at which this particular scenario affects us varies widely, but we are all subject to these types of invasions throughout life.

{ Who Hurts Us? }

The short answer to the question "Who hurts us?" is everyone. Whether you are an even-tempered person who is not easily disturbed, or a hypersensitive individual who tends to take the actions of others a little too personally, you will be hurt, offended, disgusted, and disturbed by many different people.

Some of them, as mentioned earlier, will be total strangers, and others will be our closest loved ones. We spend a great deal of time trying to get from one place to another in our lives. We go to and from work, recreational activities, vacation, and school functions; we are always on the move. We have to leave our nesting areas in order to get the things we need. Meanwhile, there are millions of other people in a hurry, trying to do the same thing.

How many times have you driven away from the gas station a little more frustrated than when you pulled in? Someone may cut you off because they somehow believe their need for gas is more urgent and more important than yours. Or, the clerk inside is having a bad day, and he is intent on making sure everyone else has a bad day, also.

There is an important point that should be mentioned here before we look a little deeper into the issue of who hurts us. There is really no such thing as insignificant pain. No matter how, why, or to what degree your world has been disrupted, the issue needs to be addressed sooner or later, because the accumulation of even the seemingly insignificant offenses have a negative impact.

In today's world, you don't even have to be in any particular location in order to run into confrontation. Unless you live in the Sahara Desert, you have probably had some bad experiences while simply driving down the road. The effects of these accumulated experiences are being seen more often, as they manifest into what is now called road rage.

The work place is, no doubt, one of the easiest places to pick up resentment. We spend much of our lives at work. The job can be a constant source of pressure, stress, and competition. The unique combination of personalities, backgrounds, agendas, and work ethic can all come together to set up a hostile environment.

Employment can be difficult to obtain, and changing jobs is a risky and nerve-racking endeavor. It is not unusual for a person to end up feeling trapped in a job, stuck with people that are difficult to deal with, and having to deal with them on a daily basis. If you have a supervisor who is not a people-person, then you could find that dealing with the people at work takes more energy than the job itself.

School is another arena that is filled with potential hardship. We interact with fellow students from the elementary grades on to the completion of our schooling. In this arena, there is an endless potential for negative experiences that can have long-term consequences.

If you ask people who had the greatest influence on their lives outside of their immediate family, many will speak of a teacher who helped shape their lives. Teachers are extremely important, but largely unappreciated and shamefully underpaid. If you look at the responsibility they have and compare it to the amount of money they take home, it becomes clear that it takes a special person to become an educator. Teachers have a real influence on the youth of America, but, unfortunately, they are not immune to the defects that are part of our nature, and they, too, can cause great destruction in the hearts and minds of young people.

{ The More You Have Invested, The More It Hurts }

If we are to experience all that is available with respect to relationships, and connect with people in ways that are much more than simple or superficial, then we will have to open ourselves up in ways that make the potential for being hurt much greater.

Significant bonds can only be built through trust. The beauty of relationships is that the more you trust and the more you are willing to give of yourself, the deeper the relationship can be. Actually, the amount of trust you have in a person is directly related to how much of yourself you are willing to give. Only when we feel safe are we able to open up and give of ourselves in a manner that can lead to a rewarding relationship.

There are some risks involved with making the level of commitment necessary to enjoy full and complete relationships with friends, family, and spouses. When we welcome others into our lives and hearts, we must let our defenses down, and, in doing so, we leave ourselves exposed and vulnerable. It really is a double-edged sword. If we don't open up and give of ourselves, we will miss out on endless possibilities. But, if we let down the protective walls, then we may be invaded and suffer the consequences of taking the risk.

So we are stuck in the life-long dilemma of whom to trust, when to trust, and how much of ourselves to give. What makes finding the proper balance even tougher is the fact that we head into each encounter with full knowledge of the dangers and old tapes of past experiences playing in our heads.

Whether we know it or not, there is a tape machine in each of our heads, which is always on, and it records all painful incidents. Our mind keeps each one on file and is forever ready to play the tapes back to us, in an attempt to detour us from making the same mistakes over and over. Some people pay too close attention to the tapes, and others would do well to pay a little more attention.

The potential cost of seeking and maintaining a healthy and productive relationship can eventually outweigh the possible rewards, if we are not equipped to deal with the pain and losses that will occur along the way.

{ Leftover Childhood }

Some of our deepest wounds and longest lasting resentments may be connected to our parents. Some of our parents are still alive; some have passed on; and some people have never met one or even both of their parents. A lot of people have serious regrets and/or unresolved resentments where parents are concerned.

The residual pain people carry as a result of their childhoods varies widely from person to person, but there are some common threads that tie all of our experiences together. The hurt you feel is real; it runs deep and it can last a lifetime. That much tends to remain consistent in most situations. In the coming chapters, we will look at why we need to release old resentments, how to go about it, and what kind of results we can expect from our efforts.

{ When Do We Grow Up? }

Most people grow up, move out of their parents' homes, fall in love, and live happily ever after. At least, that is how the fairy tale goes. In reality, when we leave home, we take all of our baggage with us; then, we get married and begin a whole new journey, filled with its own pleasures and pains.

Marriage is a serious undertaking. How many other lifelong covenants does a person make? A relationship of this magnitude takes a willingness to uphold your commitment in and through all circumstances. Forgiveness plays a major role in determining whether or not a marriage survives. Open communication is a key factor, as well; without it, the marriage is not likely to be fruitful. If two people are indeed made "one" in marriage, then when you give of yourself, who are you really giving to?

We are all going to be disappointed, disrespected, and unappreciated by the ones we love, but we continue to invest in love, confident that in the long run the rewards will outweigh the costs.

{ Why We Get Hurt }

We all get into each other's way as everyone seeks to fulfill his own needs. There are so many factors that are out of our control. Other people often do not have your best interest at heart. They have their own issues of stored-up fear and anger from dysfunctional backgrounds. Not stepping on others' toes is not a priority on most people's agenda. People can totally derail your day and not give it a second thought or even recognize their wrongdoing if confronted. Many people are going to live and be motivated by selfishness. There is no way of changing that fact, nor should we want to. You can't change the weather, either, but you can dress appropriately to meet the conditions, and in doing so, put yourself in a position of not feeling the effects so strongly.

One of the chief reasons we get hurt is because we set ourselves up for pain. In relationships, we tend to expect the other party to think, act, and respond in a manner similar to our own. The world would be a better place if people would just do what we expect them to do, but the truth is that people are not going to conform to our expectations, nor are they supposed to. The lack of open communication and the presence of unreasonable expectations are probably the greatest causes of disappointment and hardship in our attempt to find and keep a partner. These same factors also contribute to the overall poor health of many relationships.

There are enough forces working against us that we must be careful not to get in our own way. So much of what happens is out of our control that we need to take care in the choices we make concerning the things that are within our circle of influence. When people hurt us, we can compound the problem by turning around and hurting ourselves. Most of the time, when someone hurts us, we are the ones that spend all of the time and energy stewing over it. They have long since moved on and are not at all affected by all of the turmoil in our minds.

Life is full of tests and painful situations that are actually wonderful opportunities to grow. That may sound a little strange, but it is true. We can and should benefit from our past experiences. Learning from the past will set us up for healthy futures. So learning to deal with, as well as work through the pain others create in our lives may be a burden, but it will have very real and long-lasting rewards.

CHAPTER 3

WHAT FORGIVENESS IS AND WHAT IT ISN'T

{ Benny's Box }

If you watch children as they play in a sandbox in the back yard of any neighborhood, you will see before long exactly who owns the sandbox. The owner of the sandbox is the one who makes up the rules, which are subject to change without notice or negotiation. The owner is also in charge of determining when a rule has been violated; lastly, he alone sits in judgment of what the appropriate punishment will be for the violator. Continued disruptive behavior and rule violations can result in banishment from the sandbox.

In essence, the owner of the sandbox is the king of his domain. He is the legislator, the law enforcement, and the judge, all in one, with absolute power, at least until his mother calls him in for lunch.

Let's take a look inside one particular back yard at a specific sandbox. Benny is the young king of this domain, and his actions indicate he is fully aware of the fact that he is in charge of everything inside his box. Nowhere else is he more comfortable and more in control than inside his private sandbox.

As we watch Benny interact with one of the other neighborhood children, it might make you wonder if selfishness is an inherent part of our nature or a learned behavior. If it is a learned behavior, then it is one we humans are able to pick up and master very quickly in life.

On some occasions, Benny's mother will take him to the park where there is a large public sandbox. It is critical to be properly prepared before embarking on a venture to the big sandbox. Benny is very careful to bring the right equipment. He needs a good bucket and strong shovel for trench-digging. He will also need a couple of armored vehicles for troop transportation and launching attacks on local enemies. In addition, he carries two pockets filled with plastic army men to place around his perimeter to help ward off invaders.

On the way to the park, his mother gives him the usual speech about playing fairly with the other kids and treating them the way he wants to be treated. Benny's mother is always talking to him about an important man named Jesus and telling him how Jesus teaches people that it is better to give than to receive.[2] His mother is trying to teach him a wonderful spiritual truth, but young Benny doesn't know Jesus, and he can't understand how giving away his stuff could be a good thing. Benny's mother insists, "Through giving, you actually receive more than you give." None of that makes any sense to Benny. He figures that Jesus's dad must be rich, and therefore He can afford to give away His toys.

Doesn't his mother understand that out there in the big sandbox, it is every man for himself? It's all about staking out your territory and then defending it; everyone knows that. If, by chance, someone leaves himself in a vulnerable position, then it is your duty to attack and gain more territory. The objective is to obtain, defend, and, when possible, attack. If you start sharing and giving, you will be invaded and quickly overrun, ending up with nothing. Benny knows the unwritten rules of the sandbox well and practices them with great enthusiasm.

{ A Grown Up Box }

Let's fast-forward about twenty-five years and look in on Benny. It could be said that, in many ways, there haven't been a lot of fundamental changes in Benny's life. His personal sandbox has gotten bigger and so have his toys, but he has retained many of the same mindsets, which have always motivated his actions.

Benny is a hard-working and fiercely independent man. He takes great pride in the fact that he owes no man and he has never needed anyone's help. He has staked out his own territory and enjoys ruling over his kingdom. He never asks for assistance and rarely offers it. He does participate in various charitable activities around town, so he does not appear as if he is not doing his civic duty, but he is just going through the motions, for the most part. Benny is a good man who is committed to his family. He is a responsible husband, father, and provider. He has even built a sandbox in his own back yard for his two little girls to play in. Now, they can learn the same valuable lessons he did about the rules of the sandbox.

On most Saturdays, Benny can be found out in front of his house, tending to the yard or working on one of his vehicles. There is always a lot for Benny to do in order to keep everything in his "sandbox" organized and working properly.

Across the street from Benny lives an elderly man named Jim. Jim retired from the restaurant business a number of years ago and took up fishing for a hobby. He has a small boat that he keeps strapped to the top of his car. For a few years, he would go fishing almost everyday, but now he can't quite get up the energy to go. The neighborhood children make fun of him because he keeps that old boat tied across the top of his car and everybody knows he never uses it. Jim is not a really popular guy in his neighborhood. He doesn't get invited to many back-yard barbeques. He lives his life guided by much the same philosophy as Benny. He takes care of himself and expects everyone to do the same. Oh, he makes an appearance at the local shelter to pass out food to the homeless on Thanksgiving, but that is about his only effort put forth in the service to others.

Jim spends most of his days tending to small tasks around his yard. He struggles to accomplish even the lightest of chores because of his failing health. He and Benny have lived across the street from each other for years, but they have never had more than a few words between them. Benny has noticed that Jim has difficulty taking care of his yard and other household chores. From time to time, Benny has felt the urge to offer assistance, but he always resists the urge. Benny has his own tasks to tend to, and besides, Jim would probably be offended if someone offered to help.

One fall afternoon, a Saturday, Benny is standing in the street taking a break from working on his car. He and his wife are sharing a cold drink, and they happen to notice their neighbor Jim struggling to get the leaves from his yard bagged up. Benny's wife urges him to help, but he resists. At that point his wife gives him "the look" and he knows if he wants to keep the peace he'd better get across the street and put those leaves in a bag.

Reluctantly, he walks over to Jim, not comfortable with the idea of leaving his own sandbox and going without invitation to Jim's. He meets resistance when first offering to help and quickly thinks, "Oh well, I tried." After glancing back at his wife, he decides it might be in his best interest to insist on helping Jim. So he makes it clear to Jim that he intends to stay until the work is done.

The men begin to work together, and before long, the discomfort within each man starts to subside. Pride and egos are laid aside as they fall into the rhythm of the work. Jim is no longer embarrassed by having Benny help him, and Benny finds the experience is not nearly as unpleasant as he had anticipated.

The two men talk briefly after the work is done, and Benny heads

26

home. In the short walk across the street, Benny realizes he feels oddly satisfied with having given of himself and his time. There were some awkward moments, and Benny didn't like being pushed out of his comfortable and familiar sandbox by his wife, but he was actually glad he helped, even though he didn't want to.

In one brief encounter, Benny made a wonderful discovery that eventually changed his life in many ways. He found through personal experience that his mother had indeed been right about giving. He discovered that through giving, you are rewarded in a way that is even better than receiving. It still didn't make much sense to him, but he knew it to be true.

As this chapter progresses and we look into the meaning of the word forgiveness, we will begin to see that forgiveness is an act; it is an act of giving. It is a gift you give to others (even when you don't want to) because in reality, it is a gift you give to yourself, and in the long run it is you who benefits. Forgiveness is a source of relief and freedom that is too often left untapped, because people don't understand its value.

The things which most people count as valuable often require commitment and work to obtain and maintain. In a like manner, forgiveness is a sometimes tough process that is preceded by sacrifice and then followed by closure. It doesn't matter if a person was hurt long ago or is currently being victimized in a situation beyond his control; forgiveness is what releases us from those burdens and opens a gateway to true freedom.

There is no one who can release you from the pain and frustration of being wronged except you. The most difficult aspect of forgiveness to grasp is the fact that the only way to be released from the burden is by releasing those who have caused the pain. This incomprehensible but unavoidable fact is what keeps countless people quietly stuck in their own personal prison. Forgiveness can free us and put us back in control.

There are several different types of forgiveness. Actually, a more correct statement would be that there is only one true type of forgiveness and a number of other half-measures which people mistake for forgiveness. Being indifferent about a situation is one way that people deal with things that may or may not directly influence their lives, but not to acknowledge a wrong is a shortcut to nowhere, and shortcuts lead to setbacks.

If you forgive someone, but still make a point of mentally marking his or her misdeed onto an account, then it is not real forgiveness. One reason why we keep a record of wrongs is because we just can't seem to totally let go. In addition, that information could come in handy someday; everyone knows people save coupons with the intent of one day using them.

{ The Literal Definition }

By looking at the actual definition of the word forgiveness we can learn some interesting and enlightening facts. In English, the word forgive is a verb, and involves an act of letting go, giving away, releasing, or granting relief. In forgiving, we relinquish our right to punish, and in doing so, we release ourselves; we are no longer tied to the offense. When you offer a gift to someone, you give away all rights to that object; you have chosen to do so and have proceeded willingly. The Aramaic[3] word for forgiveness means to pour out or empty. In forgiving, we pour out the pain and empty ourselves of resentment; it is a cleansing process. In the Hebrew language, the word for forgiveness can mean to clear the conscience and have confidence in the future, or getting relief from something that has carried you away. This is a good example, because we can be carried away by the effects of unforgiveness.

In ancient times, forgiveness was always associated with and preceded by sacrifice, relinquishing ownership of something completely. In order to enjoy the fruits and freedom forgiving offers, we must go through the uncomfortable and unwanted process of sacrificing our need to seek justice or revenge, and we have to let our pride die away.

In the Greek language, there are several variations to the word forgiveness: to set free; to bestow an unconditional favor; and to suspend the just penalty, whether the offense was done in ignorance or on purpose. The root word means to lose, to let go, or to release a tightened grip.

Throughout time and within many different cultures, we see again and again this same unchanging truth showing us that some of the best and most precious gifts available are related to giving before receiving.[4] There is no question that in forgiving, you have to be willing to make some sacrifices. Some old mindsets and methods of dealing with life must die away before the reward associated with your sacrifice will be realized.

{ If Forgiveness Is Good, Then Why Is It So Difficult? }

Forgiveness is not natural, so naturally, it is difficult. Humans seem to be much more inclined to demand payment when wronged than to grant a pardon. From childhood, we hear that getting even is where you will find satisfaction. An eye for an eye is true justice; with anything else, the scales are not balanced. Unfortunately, one of society's fundamental justifications for teaching and seeking retaliation, rather than giving grace, is based on one of the most widely misunderstood and inappropriately applied scriptures in the Bible. The overly quoted and rarely understood verses in the Bible which speak of an eye for an eye are clearly referring to fair compensation in personal and civil matters, not revenge.[5] That law, like many other

29

laws, was implemented to prevent escalating retaliation. It was meant to help corral and harness our natural desire to get back more than we lost. There are some traditions that we grow up with, concerning forgiveness, that make it easy for us to hold onto resentment. We somehow believe it is our right and duty not to forgive. We want justice; someone has to pay.

There are consequences to our actions; no one is debating that fact. If someone runs into your car, then you should be able to expect "fair" compensation for your loss. If you are paid for the damage incurred, then the scales are even and the issue should be resolved. But for some reason, that isn't good enough for some people. We want to remain in the discomfort caused us, seeking more than fair compensation, reliving the injustice of the event, and sharing it with anyone who will listen. We are the victims of someone else's wrong deeds, and ironically, many people like to remain the bitter victim, content with accumulating life's hardships and storing them away like some kind of trophy. We own our hardships and wear them like a badge. An example of our desire not to get too far away from our pain can be seen in the way we claim our own infirmities with a certain tone of affection, such as "my bad back" or "my arthritis." People often find identity and purpose in their problems, nurturing and perpetuating the pain, which is a sad, but true, reality.

If we are honest with ourselves, we will admit that we enjoy being mad at someone; it feels good. Being shortchanged at the hamburger stand gives us something to "bite into" and "chew on," and we enjoy every "bite." Some of the best plans for revenge are secretly played out in the mind, with every moment savored, and every step rehearsed again and again. Have you ever done that? Sure you have.

One very real, if not often discussed, reason why it is difficult to forgive is simply because it is easier and seemingly more fun not to forgive. Reliving wrongs we have endured and blaming others is a great pastime. Actually, not forgiving may appear to be fun, and it certainly appeals to our nature, but it isn't healthy. Dragging around a bag of rocks all of the time so that you will be ready to stone others will make you old before your time. There is an old Chinese proverb that says, "If you are going to seek revenge on your enemy, you better dig two graves." This paints a pretty clear picture of the eventual price of revenge.

There is one more aspect of the issue about why it is so difficult to forgive others that should be mentioned. In many cases, it can be our own unresolved issues that we allow to affect how we deal with others. Having been rejected or not forgiven for past wrongs we have committed can influence our ability and willingness to pardon others. This may be done knowingly or unknowingly, but what we are doing in these cases is passing on the pain, rather than dealing with it; the people we pass it on to are likely to be the ones we love.

{ Forgiveness Isn't... }

Forgiveness is not about becoming a doormat for someone else to walk on. Surrendering your resentments does not mean that you have accepted someone's behavior as reasonable or just. It is recognizing a wrong and then releasing yourself from the burdens of that wrong by granting a pardon to the offender.

Forgiveness does not involve taking on the blame for someone else or minimizing a situation. Everything must be looked at and dealt with in an open and honest way. Minimizing can lead to further hardships, especially in personal relationships. Trying to keep the peace is necessary and admirable, but we must be careful to not take on that role at the cost of our own well-being or the health of the relationship.

Ignoring or sidestepping a situation and acting as if things are fine is not how forgiveness works, either. Our feelings have to be acknowledged and dealt with before any issue can be resolved. Sidestepping issues is one good way to start, or continue, a cycle of enabling others to abuse us.

When the process of forgiveness is complete, there will be no inward need to receive payment from those who have hurt you and there will be no desire to bring up or rehash the situation in your mind or with others.

The idea of seeking relief by granting release to others who have harmed us may seem foreign or even offensive, because it rubs against the grain of our nature and many long standing traditions we grow up with in our culture. Unforgiveness is normal and widely accepted, but that doesn't make it right. "If I find myself in the company of the majority, it may be time for me to reform (or pause and reflect)," is a quote attributed to Mark Twain. Many people believe closure can be found on the other side of revenge or justice, but they are sadly mistaken.

{Unforgiven}

Outside the prison in Huntsville, Texas, people gather before the execution of a condemned man. Some come out of morbid curiosity; some show up to protest the death penalty; others come in support. On this particular day, there are also people present who have a very personal connection to the event. The family of the condemned man, as well as the parents of the victim, are all in attendance.

The family of the man who is to be executed for killing a store clerk during the commission of a robbery is trying to come to grips with the idea that their loved one will be taken from them shortly. They have forgiven him for the countless burdens he has placed on their hearts over the years. While they grieve their loss, they also have a deep compassion for the family of the man who was killed in this senseless tragedy. They understand as best they can the pain the victim's family must be enduring. In many ways, they know exactly what the other family is going through. Everyone on both sides of this sad story has suffered untold and incomprehensible pain.

There is a local news team on the scene, which is going through the crowd and recording interviews with different people. The reporter approaches a couple sitting quietly in their lawn chairs and asks them who they are and why they have come. The woman speaks and tells the reporter that they are the parents of the victim. No one can know or understand the anguish these people have had to live through because of the murder of their son. It is completely unfair that this couple or any parent should be subjected to this despair.

The parents of the victim have shown up in search of some kind of relief from the relentless pain. Maybe, by being here when the execution is performed, they can find what they are looking for. The reporter gently questions the mother, with the hope of recording her mental and emotional state for the cameras. The mother is clearly despondent and appears to be worn out by the weight of the burdens she has been forced to carry. The father sits in the background with a blank stare on his face, as the mother shares her pain with the reporter. She says her wonderful son, who never harmed anyone, was taken from her almost ten years ago. He was brutally murdered for no reason by the man who is about to be executed. She says, "There has been no rest in my heart since his death. We came to see the final stages of justice played out. We came here hoping to find closure."

The execution is carried out according to the law, and the condemned man is now banished from the planet forever. The scales are now even; justice has been served; but, for some reason, it just isn't as satisfying as some of the people had expected. People with broken dreams and heavy hearts walk away from the scene. The poor old couple has surely suffered enough already, but now they must get into their car and drive away with an empty and unfulfilled feeling in their stomachs.

A lot of people go to Huntsville, Texas, believing that they will find closure on the other side of what happens there, but they always drive away disappointed.

Forgiveness is all about giving grace, even when the object of your forgiveness may not be worthy of such a gift in your eyes. In forgiving, we give away our rights to punish and invoke our right to be unburdened.

The whole concept and process of forgiveness seems backwards, because it tells us we have to relinquish to receive, and we have to give in order to get. There are few areas in life where you can gain true victory through surrender, but that is how forgiveness works. It is this paradox that makes forgiving so difficult, but that is precisely why it is so valuable.

The cause of suffering in life can start outside our circle of influence, but then be perpetuated by us because of our inability or lack of willingness to deal with our pain in a healthy way. There are already enough things in life that lay outside of our ability to influence, and that is why forgiveness is such an important skill to learn and practice. Through forgiveness, we can end our own suffering, rather than increase it. No matter what life throws at us, we alone are in control of how we react. That statement gives us both freedom and responsibility.

CHAPTER 4

WHY SHOULD I FORGIVE

Everything that is physical has a beginning and an eventual end. Even the universe we live in, which stretches out beyond our imagination, did not exist at one time, and at some unknown and unfathomable point in the future, it will no longer exist. All things move in a cycle from birth to death. The galaxy where our solar system lies is thought to be in constant motion. At the center of our system is the sun, which has its own cycles, and around it, all of the planets revolve.

The earth revolves around the sun and it rotates on its own axis. It is affected by the moon, which also moves in a repetitive pattern. Each aspect of the entire system has an effect on, and is affected by, every other aspect. Together, an amazing balance is struck, with each part playing a role that contributes to the function of the system as a whole.

Here on earth, the cycle of birth, life, and death are played out again and again, each year, through life's reflection of the seasonal changes. Each season prepares the way and has an effect on the following season. The earth is cleansed and renewed by the daily movement of the tides and seasonal changes.

We are born into this system, where there are continuous cycles playing out and unfolding. It should not be a surprise to find out that part of our search for balance includes the attempt to fall into rhythm with the natural cycles of this planet.

From the navigation of the ancient mariners to the productivity of the modern farmer, success has always been dependent upon having knowledge and awareness of how each element within this complex system affects the rest of the system.

We need to know that if we expect to be able to navigate safely on our own journey through life, and have a fruitful existence, we will need to be aware of how we have been affected by life, and how in turn, we affect others. In the natural cycles of our planet, all things work together to bring balance, but in human relationships, the actions of one person can have a very negative and long lasting effect on the lives of many others. This can bring them out of balance and lead to the beginning of destructive cycles, in which dysfunction becomes normal.

{ Annie Revisited }

You may have wondered about what happened to poor little Annie, who we spent one sad day with a couple of chapters back. She is alive, if not totally well at this point of her journey. Annie has been forced to endure more hardship than most children, but sadly, her story is really not that unusual. Annie, along with countless others, has grown up in a world where abuse on many different levels and selfishness are normal. There is one ironic but sad reality to Annie's story; since she has never known anything different than the environment she grew up in, she is not totally aware of the emotional damage she has sustained. Unfortunately, she is also not aware of how that damage can and will have an impact on her future.

Annie fell in love and married early in life. Her need for love and affection was strong, and at that age, young men are willing to fulfill those needs, as long as their own superficial needs are met in the process. Young love is intense, if not enduring, so this was a pleasant time for Annie. However, it could be said that it was her past that was shaping her future, because she may have married more out of a need to escape than a need to commit to a lifelong covenant.

Some predictable problems have risen up soon enough in her marriage. She is not able to give of herself emotionally or physically in a way that is satisfying to her husband and healthy for the marriage. She is becoming much more withdrawn and isolated. Annie feels like she has no one to reach out to, and the events of her childhood make it obvious why she has developed some problems with trusting people. Now, in her marriage, because of some unresolved issues in her past, she cannot really lean on and confide in her partner. It is not her husband's fault; he has his own character defects, but he is doing the best that he can. In fact, he has not done anything that would make Annie believe she cannot trust him, yet.

It was once said, "I have experienced many terrible things in life, some of which actually happened." We have a way of creating our own reality, and if Annie believes her husband cannot be trusted, then he will pick up on that energy and eventually give her a reason not to trust him. It is as if the target of our distrust is lured into breaking our trust by our own paranoia, or maybe they just get tired of the accusations and act out in frustration.

{ A New Life }

On this day, Annie is peering down into a crib, gazing at her very own newborn daughter, whom she and her husband have just brought home from the hospital. She feels as if she has been born again. There is a new life, a new and different hope. In many ways, she can now start over and maybe have a chance to right all of the wrongs, or at least not allow her child to be subjected to the same burdens she was subject to.

Simply soaking in the beauty of her new baby, Jane, is almost overwhelming for Annie. The child is so precious and innocent that Annie can literally see the perfect love radiating from her baby daughter as she sleeps. The smell of this newborn miracle fills the room and sets well on Annie's heart. While standing next to baby Jane's bed, Annie is enveloped in peace. Surely, she is not worthy of such a gift, and yet there she is.

Despite all of her joy, Annie feels a tugging at her heart. Mixed in with the pleasure of this very special moment is fear and anxiety. How will she ever be able to give Jane everything she needs and deserves? Her own parents missed the mark, and in doing so, left her even less equipped to care for this beautiful baby than they were.

No child is born into a place that is free and clear of dysfunction. There is no such thing as a perfect parent or a perfect childhood. As Annie ponders the potential of her own failure as a parent, she suddenly realizes that her parents were far from perfect, but they too must have had baggage that was imputed upon them from their own journey through life.

Annie's parents must have gazed down on her and saw the same miracle of new life that she is looking at now, but their efforts fell short anyway. Annie now knows inside that despite her best efforts, she too will be less than perfect, and she will fail Jane in one way or another, if not in many ways.

As a mother, she is determined to promote love in her child's life and is committed to doing her best to instill a spirit of trust and giving. She can only hope that her own child will one day be able to appreciate her efforts, understand that all people make mistakes, and forgive her in the areas in which she falls short.

Sometimes, we have to be confronted with our own failures before we are willing to look at the failures of others in a different way. Annie now knows that in order to prevent her past from consuming her future, she will have to first forgive her parents and then begin her own healing process. That is what is best for her and for her precious baby.

Before Annie leaves Jane's bedside, she stops and prays that God will protect and guide her new baby onto the right paths and allow her life to proceed according to His will.

{ Leaving The Past Behind }

Annie now lives with the freedom she gained by releasing the burdens of her past. Having taken an open and honest look at her own shortcomings is one thing that helps her to forgive others when their words or actions are harmful. Her daughter Jane is now a young woman who is spending her second year in college away from home. Although Annie has some regrets, and there have been some tough times between her and Jane, they have a healthy relationship that has benefited them both in ways they will never totally comprehend.

On this day, Annie finds herself once again standing in Jane's bedroom. The crib has long since been stored away, and the room has taken on many different looks over the years, but she can still smell the scent of her baby daughter lingering, that same smell that began their bond so many years ago. Annie finishes cleaning up and closes the door behind her.

Jane is spending the summer overseas, in India, doing some missionary work with a Christian youth group to which she belongs. Annie struggled with the idea of her daughter going on this trip for a number of reasons. Naturally, she would prefer that Jane be at home this summer, and going to a foreign country can be dangerous. Annie has found some consolation in the fact that she is going to fly over and spend a week with Jane to support her in her endeavor to help others.

During her trip overseas, Annie finds that just trying to get to her destination is a difficult feat. The area where her daughter is working is hot and miserable. The air is muggy and almost too thick to breathe. There are no luxuries in this place, not even the things most people would consider necessary to sustain life. How could anyone survive here, and why would her daughter want to be in this desolate environment? It is as inhospitable a place as there could ever be, and yet there are people everywhere, all living in total depravity. The sights and smells are overwhelming.

Annie goes with Jane one morning to help bring some assistance to the local people. They are trying to gather the children and provide some basic medical care for them. As the day wears on, there is a point when Annie notices her daughter working just below her, kneeling down in the mud, ministering to the needs of a child. As Annie gazes down on her daughter, time stands still. In her mind's eye, she can see and even smell her daughter as a newborn, lying in her crib sleeping. She remembers her hopes and fears as she peered down into Jane's crib, and right now, she knows without a doubt that the prayer she sent to God the very first night she brought Jane home has been answered.

It is a very humbling and extremely rewarding moment that never would have happened if Annie did not have the wisdom to forgive her own parents and stop the cycle of destruction.

[Our Actions Have A Lasting Effect]

As each of us passes through this life, a remnant of who we are will be left behind. Certainly, in our children there is a genetic remnant, but also, in the hearts and minds of those with whom we had contact, there is a residual effect.

What do you want to be a reflection of? What impact do you want to have on the people you come in contact with, especially your loved ones? Who do you have in your life that you want to be there for in the best possible way? These are questions we need to ask ourselves from time to time in order to help gain and maintain a proper perspective. Remembering we have a definite impact on others is also a good reason to stay motivated in the area of forgiveness.

Forgiveness is an investment that always pays dividends. As we have just witnessed in Annie's story, it can open up new channels for success in relationships and help us to give and receive love on levels never experienced. Why would we cheat ourselves and possibly others out of such great potential by staying stuck in unforgiveness in any area of our lives?

{ What Is Resentment Worth? }

To open up new avenues and expose ourselves to new experiences is one reason to be committed to forgiveness in all seasons, but let's look at the question "Why should I forgive?" from another angle.

Exactly what is it that we gain by not forgiving? As tightly as we tend to hold onto unforgiveness, one would think it has some significant value, but in reality that just isn't the case. We somehow believe we are maintaining control by holding on to resentment, when in fact, the opposite is what occurs. By holding onto any unforgiveness, we are giving control to that situation or person. We are, in effect, honoring that person or situation by allowing them to occupy space in our mind.

Whether it is a minor incident or a major blow, a situation from our past or a present burden, it doesn't make sense to allow someone else to rent space in our head. Why should we allow anything to have a continued negative effect in our lives? People carry around resentments that are decades old; what good has that ever served?

{ How's Your Hamster Wheel? }

Have you ever watched a hamster get on the wheel in its cage? It seems to love jumping on the wheel and running. It can spend a lot of time on the wheel, but when it stops, no real progress has been made. This is a great picture of what we do when we get upset. We get on our own personal hamster wheel and start running, reliving a situation over and over, projecting different outcomes, and playing out different scenarios. We love our hamster wheels; everyone has one, and most people use them regularly. The wheel is standard equipment; it comes with the cage, so why not use it? The hamster wheel's use is not limited to issues concerning forgiveness; we get on it and try to run toward solutions involving money, employment, and schooling, and the list goes on and on. The wheel also goes wherever we go; it can be used in the car or at work, and it comes with a lifetime guarantee.

We not only enjoy using our own hamster wheel; we also like watching others as they use their own. However, spending time on the hamster wheel or observing others as they run toward nowhere is not considered healthy recreational activity, nor is it considered real exercise. It is an exercise in futility, at best, and can lead the mind into some dangerous places.

{ Forgiveness, The Total Package }

Forgiveness can have a positive influence on all aspects of your life. Better overall emotional, physical, and spiritual health can be obtained through the regular practice of releasing the things that bind us up and bog us down.

There are a number of spiritual truths that are either directly or indirectly connected to forgiveness. We have already covered the idea that it is better to give than to receive. At first glance, this may seem to be some old religious teaching that is emphasized in an attempt to get people to support a specific church or religion, but there is so much more to this amazing truth than what we traditionally believe it to be. It may also appear to be a way for parents to teach their children a lesson about sharing and instilling in them good habits, which it is in part; but again, it is so much more.

It requires a level of maturity to be able to understand, practice, and appreciate the idea of receiving through giving. But how can we get to a point of really appreciating and using this beautiful truth, when so often it is used to manipulate people through fear and guilt, in an attempt to govern what some people consider to be morality, when in fact morality cannot be governed?

This spiritual truth is meant to be experienced and shared on a personal level. It has no real value as an offensive weapon or manipulation tactic. Forcing it down people's throats or beating them over the head with it will never result in giving anyone a deeper understanding of its beauty. Living this truth is the only way to experience it or share it with others. We can either choose to abide by this truth or ignore it, but the truth itself will always remain the same. Forgiveness could actually be looked at as a selfish act, because the one who forgives is the one who receives the true reward.

{ A Look At The Physical To Help See The Spiritual }

There are many physical laws that govern the world we live in. Gravity is one good example of a physical truth that remains the same regardless of our actions. The person who recognizes, respects, and abides by the physical laws that govern our world is naturally going to live a happier and healthier life. If you choose to ignore the reality of gravity, there will be consequences; the same can be said about spiritual truths.

The scripture that says you have to forgive in order to be forgiven[6] is absolutely true, but like so many other spiritual truths, it is often misunderstood. This spiritual law does not involve the balancing of some invisible scales before you are worthy of forgiveness, and it is not about using fear to motivate us into doing the right thing. This truth is not concerned with governing our actions; it is an invitation and opportunity to open and soften our hearts, and, in turn, our hearts will govern our actions. Grabbing onto and practicing this truth is important, because where a person's heart is has everything to do with what direction his life will take. A person's attitude influences his actions, and actions determine direction.

It could also be said that it is in our best interest to forgive, because what we send out in life is generally what we get back. A rough example of this principle can be seen, in a natural sense, by examining the life of a dolphin. The dolphin uses a sophisticated sonar system to send out sound waves that interact with the environment and then return back to them. The dolphin is receptive to the frequency of these waves upon their return because they are, in fact, the same waves it sent out. The dolphin sends out these waves and then uses the returning waves to gather all the information it needs to navigate, feed, and live safely in its environment. There are countless sound waves and differing frequencies that surround a dolphin at any given time, but the only ones that have a direct effect on its life and actions are the ones that it first sent out. In a similar fashion, that which we send out will always have a direct effect on our lives.

Have you ever noticed that some people are easy to spend time with and pleasant to be around, but others seem to drain your energy when you are in their presence? That is because a person's attitude, which he projects, influences the atmosphere around him. It has an effect on others and eventually has an effect on him, good or bad.

In life, it is our outlook that often determines the outcome in any situation. Forgiveness changes not only our attitude about a given situation, but can also influence our overall outlook, freeing us from old mindsets and giving us better emotional balance.

{ Stuck In The Cage }

As a bird sits in a cage, it is able to look outside its confined area, but it is not free to experience life beyond its current condition unless some changes occur. If you were to open the door of the cage and invite the bird to fly around the house, what would it do? In some cases, it may not want to leave. The cage has worked so far; why change? In some cases, it may venture outside its comfort zone and see what lies on the other side of the bars, only to quickly return to the safety of the cage when things get too uncomfortable. What about the final case, where the bird never even notices that the door is open and always has been?

Statistics show that over half of the people who are paroled from prison will eventually do something which will lead them back to prison. In many cases, they will be back in a very short time. The causes and reasons for this alarming fact are deep and complex, but one reality about human nature can be derived from this: we fall into destructive cycles and then get used to being there, becoming comfortable in our misery. Forgiveness can help us get out of the cage and help us stay out.

Through forgiveness, we are given a unique opportunity to obtain a deeper knowledge of ourselves. We gain a new awareness of how and why certain actions or words affect us. Forgiveness dictates that we take an honest look at all situations, and through these personal introspections, new discoveries will be made and useful tools obtained. Some people go through life not knowing any more than the fact that

45

something isn't right. Why not dig a little deeper? We owe ourselves that much.

We can and should be able to walk away from any encounter with a greater knowledge of self and a better understanding of others, especially when it comes to the relationships we have with the people we love and care about.

Some of life's most valuable lessons seem to come on the tail end of our greatest hardships. Learning to deal with and walk through the pain others create in our lives and the pain we create for ourselves can be a burden, but it does have very real rewards.

When someone we love hurts us, the intensity and duration of the pain can seem unbearable. When we are in the pain, there is no end in sight, and forgiveness is the last thing on our minds. But taking the right steps at this point can leave any relationship in better shape after the event than before. This really doesn't seem logical in theory, and certainly, while we are enduring the pain created by someone else, it doesn't appear to be very practical in application, either. But forgiveness is a process, and just like the unwavering spiritual truths we have discussed, it tends to look and work in a way that is backward to our natural way of thinking.

It has been said, "The strongest evidence of love is sacrifice." Sacrifice is not only evidence of love, but it is only through sacrifice that we are able to experience true love. When two people are committed to a relationship, forgiveness can help each person hold themselves and the other accountable. If you know that running away from or ignoring a situation is not an option, that eventually you will have to work through any and all problems, then that very commitment will help prevent you from doing or saying offensive things to begin with. Forgiveness promotes love, and love promotes forgiveness. They are forever working together to strengthen our relationships.

Hardships, whether caused by others or created by ourselves, can and should eventually add substance to our lives and relationships. We can reflect back on the process after it has passed and see the effort was worth it, gaining strength in the present and hope for the future.

Forgiveness in all areas of our lives, from the incident at the gas station, to when we have our hearts totally broken, can help prevent us from accumulating useless and potentially harmful baggage.

You must have long range goals to keep you from being frustrated by short term failures. Forgiveness may start out as something we learn and can clearly see as something we need to do. In its practice, it may often be a burdensome task we know we have to do, but eventually it will rest in our hearts as something we want to do.

CHAPTER 5

THE CONSEQUENCES OF NOT FORGIVING

{ A Look At Life Outside Of The Town Of Closure }

If you ever want to get a fairly accurate view of what the current personal and political opinions of the general public are, all you have to do is watch the local news. When reporters are in the field, recording the impromptu reactions of people after any newsworthy event, you can gain some insight into just what their overall outlook on life embodies. It is easy to see what people value during times of tragedy.

In one recent situation, there was a very large fire that swept through a community. The fire raged for days and laid waste to everything in its path. There were untold acres of land destroyed and over a thousand structures devastated, many of which were private homes.

As the fire died out, people were able to return to their homes, and naturally the news cameras went along for the ride. The news reports allowed others who had not been affected by the fire to huddle in their homes and peer into the lives of the people who had been.

Pictures of people sifting through the ashes, looking for some pieces of their lost world were on every channel. There were some heartwarming stories of rescue and moving testimonies of people's resolve to rebuild despite the setback. One widow found a picture of her husband in the pile of rubble that used to be her home. The unity of family could be seen on one channel, as a man with tear-filled eyes hugged his children, and made a powerful statement about how having his family all safe is what is really important. Their value to him far exceeded the value of material loss and made the loss of his home seem insignificant.

Story after story poured out of the television for days. All told, there were some heroic efforts and inspiring stories that came out of the tragedy. But there was also an alarming percentage of people affected by the fire whose focus was not on community, rebuilding, or family. Most of the people interviewed were not counting their blessings or looking forward to a renewed future. They were looking for somebody to blame. Apparently, the fire was started as a result of arson. Miles away, in a different town, someone started the fire that grew to unimaginable proportions and made victims of countless people.

The focus of many people is clearly on payback. Again and again, the camera recorded the victims' desire to find and punish whoever is responsible. One man stated there isn't enough of the guilty person to go around in order to satisfy everyone's need for justice. He says, "They should kill him and his family, and that still wouldn't pay for the loss we have suffered."

These people were clearly in the process of grieving their loss, so it is understandable that many of them were caught between disbelief and anger. Hopefully, with time, they will move from anger into and through sadness, and then find their way to acceptance.

If the interviews are any indication, it is likely that far too few of the victims will put forth the effort to move past anger to acceptance and eventually to closure, by spending some time in forgiveness. Getting to closure can be a tough task and a tall order. Just getting to a place of acceptance is work enough for most of us. Why bother with this whole idea of forgiveness and talk of closure, when it would be much more gratifying to see the person responsible caught and held accountable for all of the pain created? Maybe they should put him on public display and let all of the people throw rocks at him. Then everyone could go back to the rebuilding of their homes, feeling better about the situation, knowing that someone has paid for disrupting so many lives and causing so much damage.

Obviously, those statements are a bit extreme, but they were made to illustrate a point. Should your eventual peace in any given situation hinge on whether or not someone is made to pay for hurting you? This is a difficult question. One would naturally hope the person responsible in the case of the fire, or any situation where people are victimized, would be held accountable, but should anyone's inner peace rely on whether or not that ever happens?

That question is likely to provoke a number of different answers; the most common one is "yes"; justice must be served to complete the healing process. We, as a people, tend to believe it is our right and our duty to not forgive those who have wronged us, especially when it is an unknown "bad guy" who has perpetrated a crime against us. We need to get past the idea that in forgiving, we are doing a favor for the other person. The person who started the fire does not care who does or does not forgive him.

The person hurting us does not have to be a stranger. Even in situations where the person creating the pain is a loved one, for some reason, we have difficulty totally letting go of our need to be compensated. The bigger the infraction against us, the more reluctant we are to let go of the strangely satisfying anger that stirs inside. We never realize or care about the fact that holding onto resentment may be fashionable and it may feel good, but there is always a price to pay.

Most likely, the one holding onto the resentment is the one who pays the price.

The price paid for not forgiving is sometimes obvious and easy to see, and sometimes subtle, but it is always consistent in that every area of our lives are affected. There can be a negative impact on our spiritual, mental, emotional, and physical health when we insist on accumulating, rather than releasing, resentments.

{ The Law Is The Law }

It has been said and is certainly written in the scriptures that how you judge others is how you will be judged.[7] This is not some scare tactic that has been sent down from God in an attempt to intimidate or manipulate people into being nice to each other. This spiritual reality is not an expression of the theory of "cause and effect," nor is it insinuating God is keeping score so He can get even later. The beautiful irony of this principle is that if we judge others as not being worthy of forgiveness, then, in effect, we have judged ourselves as not being worthy of forgiveness either, because we cannot receive what we are not willing to give. It works in concert with, and parallel to, the simple truth that you cannot give what you do not possess.

This spiritual law, like all physical and spiritual laws, remains true regardless of whether we recognize and abide by it or not. There is no way to break this law; we may be broken by it or suffer the consequences of not heeding its truth, but we can no more break this law than we can break the law of gravity.

Sadly, when we are hurt, there is the initial pain that must be absorbed, but then we can compound or escalate the pain by not dealing with it properly. The result can leave us in a place where we are not able to give and receive love in ways that are useful and healthy.

Communication is important in processing all that life throws at us, but when we refuse to forgive, or use selective forgiveness, we cut off lines of communication. Many times, we can cut off communication with the very source and/or people who help us maintain balance. Open and honest inner communication with ourselves is also imperative for good mental health, and unforgiveness will surely disrupt the use of this important coping skill.

{ The Price We Pay }

Negative mindsets lead to distorted mental perceptions and can leave people focusing on the wrong things, while not giving time and energy to that which we know needs to be focused on. Being disconnected spiritually, not communicating properly with others, and having a lack of focus can all add up to a number of less than productive realities, one of them being missed opportunities. Relationships, personal and spiritual growth, employment: all of these things take commitment and energy. But how can we hope to be successful at these endeavors if we are bound up and bogged down because we are dragging around useless baggage?

Our emotional well-being is directly connected with how we deal with the actions of others. Forgiveness can be the difference between achieving victory or remaining a victim. Accumulated pain has a lasting impact on our willingness and ability to make commitments in personal relationships. Issues of trust can develop, becoming attached to our minds, and they are difficult to dislodge. Through all of this, it is never the object of our unforgiveness that suffers; we are the ones who suffer, along with anyone whom we may have a relationship with in the future.

A general attitude of "who cares?" can be common when discussing the subject of unforgiveness. The answer to the question "who cares?" should be "we do," because we are the ones who pay the price of our own unforgiveness. The effect of unresolved issues in life can be slow and subtle, like that of smoking, but like smoking, it all adds up and the eventual cost may be severe.

Unforgiveness disrupts the natural process of grieving. Whenever we suffer a loss or any disruption to our balance, there is a process or path the mind follows to help restore balance. Even on the smallest level, this principle can be demonstrated. If you are standing in line with several other people at the Department of Motor Vehicles, and the worker at the window suddenly closes the window without notice or explanation, then you have just been knocked slightly off balance. At this point, there are some predictable emotions that will occur before you are able to regain your balance. The process happens in four basic stages. First, you can't believe he just shut the window. The next emotion is likely to be anger, as you think to yourself, "How dare he shut that window on me." The third thought or emotion will be sadness, because you are disappointed the window is shut. The final stage will be when you accept the fact that the window is closed and you must move on. At this point, you need to move towards the end of the only other available line, and since you are at the DMV, you had better move quickly through these four stages. If you get stuck too long in any of these four stages, everyone in the line will beat you to the new line.

It should be pointed out that just because you have accepted the inevitable and moved on to the next line does not necessarily mean that you have released the negative energy that can be associated with being at the DMV. It may sound silly, but it will be necessary to forgive the person who closed the window and started the brief but uncomfortable event into motion. If you do not forgive him, he will be joining you on the way home. Going to the DMV can provide a great opportunity to use our hamster wheel on the drive home.

{ Even Your Body Is Affected }

We have countless encounters that are similar to the example above throughout life. The mental and emotional stress associated with day-to-day living can eventually take a toll on the body if a conscious effort is not made to take in, process, and release life's burdens. If you factor in the additional strain placed on us by trying to maintain personal relationships and the losses that must be endured along the way, it becomes easy to see how we get out of balance.

Our mental, emotional, and spiritual well-being all have a direct effect on our physical health. For years now, it has been known that the mind has an impact on the functions of the body. From some of the early work done in the field of biofeedback to the latest research, the conclusion of the scientific community is that our physical health is influenced in part by our state of mental and emotional well-being. The body does not run in a way that is separate from, and therefore, not impacted by our thoughts and emotions as it was once believed. The stresses of life place a burden not only on our minds, but on our bodies as well.

By holding onto negative thoughts, we create adverse physiological reactions in our bodies. The mind and body are trying to work in concert, so naturally, when one is strained, the other will be affected. Trouble can begin when mental stresses add up and run the body down. Once the body is run down, it will, in turn, influence us on a mental and emotional level; the outcome is a continuous cycle of poor overall health. It is not hard to see how all aspects of our health are woven together and each one affects the other.

Unforgiveness causes stress that can begin to place a strain on the body. Tension results in chemical changes within us. Some of our internal systems are put on alert and the body produces a chemical reaction that is similar to the fight-or-flight response, which the body goes into when we encounter perceived danger.

Certain systems in the body are overworked, while others are all but shut down during periods of prolonged stress and tension. The overproduction of some chemicals and underproduction of others causes toxins to build up, which will then have to be eliminated. While the body is struggling to find balance and trying to deal with the internal chemical warfare, the immune system can begin to fail. This, in turn, will further complicate the problem and place a greater strain on the system.

The short-term effects of this battle may leave a person feeling beat up, but the long-term effects can be serious. Prolonged stress on any system will eventually produce function failure. Digestive disorders, heart disease, and even cancer have been linked to stress, and few things in life cause more stress than accumulated and unresolved resentments.

Dealing with the possible physical consequences of carrying around more than our share of burdensome baggage is only one of many potential hazards we may face. While the mind is busy allowing outside forces to put the body into physiological chaos, some other adverse reactions can also be taking place. Depression is another common symptom of prolonged strain on the mind and body. It is remarkable how we can continue to operate under the conditions that we go through and create for ourselves. It is a testimony to the durability of the human mind and body, but it isn't necessary to burden ourselves and our bodies in this way.

If everything already discussed isn't bad enough, there is also a host of destructive behavior patterns and dangerous cycles people fall into everyday, in an attempt to relieve the discomfort of internal pain; all of these have their own set of potential consequences.

It is normal and natural to want to escape pain; the problem lies within the type of methods used in seeking relief. One method is to store it up and then dump it all out at one time. The problem with this particular coping skill is that there is no way of knowing when our stored anger will come out or in what fashion.

Have you ever found yourself in a situation where a minor incident may have occurred, but your level of frustration is, for some reason, much greater than logic would dictate? Have you ever overreacted when someone offends you? When we store up, rather than deal with and release frustration, sooner or later those feelings will surface. Unfortunately, whoever is around when our "frustration tank" is full can expect to receive more than his share of our displeasure. Aggressions rising up and then being displaced upon others is a predictable manifestation of stored resentment. This can become an established pattern for releasing unresolved issues. In its worst form, victims of physical abuse are created. In a milder, but just as unhealthy version, we see the person who stores up everything that life dishes out, and then regularly dumps it on some undeserving person, usually a loved one.

Stored anger doesn't have to come out in the form of violence for people to get hurt. Too many harmful words are thrown at the people we love, because we are unable or unwilling to work through all that comes across our path by forgiving or using constructive communication. Our loved ones may not mind assisting us in processing our frustrations by acting as a "sounding board" from time to time, but they do not deserve to be abused.

Rather than store up pain, some people lean toward one of the cover-up methods for dealing with discomfort. Some people pour alcohol on their issues, and others might try to poison the pain out of their system with various types of illegal and prescription drugs. Some attempt to eat their way to closure and others try starvation. Some chase money and some spend money; the list goes on and on.

The obsessions, addictions, and self-destructive cycles associated with attempts to relieve pain are widespread and cross over every economic and cultural line in our society. The places people will go in search of relief are remarkable. Our negative thoughts carry with them a certain energy that drives negative actions, which create destructive patterns ending in habits that can imprison people for life.

All of these unhealthy coping skills have certain things in common. They hurt, rather than help, the people using them, and they hurt the people around those who use them. They do not deal with pain, they do not relieve pain, and they do not lead to closure.

{ A Short Trip From The Stage To The Toilet }

Jack and Diane were young sweethearts who shared an intense love for each other. They were emotionally connected early in life and experienced many firsts together. She came from a family that was dysfunctional long before the term was fashionable. Divorce, dissension, death, and suicide were all part of Diane's reality. She was a quiet, young beauty who needed a hero, and Jack happened along at the right time. Jack grew up in a family where the father was a man's man, and the mother committed her energy to the physical needs of her children, while quietly struggling with her own issues of self worth and purpose.

Jack was a popular boy with a rebel's heart and enough talent, good looks, and personality to pretty much have things his own way. Their bond was strong; Diane found security in his confidence, and Jack found someone to accept all of his youthful love. They were happy beyond expression and carried with them an inward assurance of success, as they packed up and moved out into the world, deeply in love, but terribly blind to the hazards that lay straight ahead.

They were not too far down the road before it became evident that Jack was totally ignorant about the emotional needs of his wife. He didn't have any idea what a woman needed, and if she was trying to communicate her needs, he must have been tuned into the wrong station. Jack thought providing for his family and being home for dinner on time was how he was supposed to meet Diane's needs.

In marriage, the best way to get your own needs met is to make a priority of meeting the needs of your partner. For the most part, that is what Diane did, and what Jack thought he was doing. Jack didn't know he had his own emotional needs, so he was in no position to provide for the deeper needs of Diane. With Diane's background, she needed to be nurtured in a way she did not understand herself, and therefore, could not express to her husband.

The intensity of their youthful love wore off, and the reality of human nature set in. Jack was so shallow that he had a habit of taking everyone for granted. He spent too much time trying to be a man and not enough trying to be a husband and father. He was at least aware enough to know he should be making a greater attempt to please his wife, but his selfishness kept him busy pursuing far too many activities that were pushing Diane away.

Jack's arrogance and ignorance combined, and left him blind to the reality that Diane had drifted away and was no longer committed to the marriage. He had his suspicions, but that wasn't new; he was always jealous and hesitant to trust.

When Diane dropped the bomb on Jack, he was not prepared for a failure of that magnitude. It was beyond his ability to comprehend; they were life-long partners, so how could she just quit? That was impossible. So started Jack's process of trying to regain his balance after having his legs cut out from under him. There was a long and painful road ahead for Jack. He stayed in disbelief far too long, and did not do himself any favors while he was there. Then he moved onto anger, and spent a lot of time on his hamster wheel. Constantly envisioning the man who had taken his place sitting on what used to be his couch, feet propped up on the coffee table he had built, watching his TV, while the woman who was once his wife prepared this stranger a meal in the kitchen. While running on his hamster wheel day after day, Jack couldn't shake the picture in his mind of another man lying with Diane. This reoccurring thought was so agonizing that sometimes he thought his head might explode; the pain was unbearable.

Jack slipped into a depression that lay on him with great force. He went to every dark corner on the planet seeking relief, but only found more pain. He got stuck in the maddening cycle of staggering from anger to depression and then over to revenge, and then starting all over again.

He couldn't even get to acceptance and probably really did not want to. Accepting responsibility for his predicament, accepting the position his actions had put Diane in, and accepting her decision was more than he could do.

He eventually accepted she was really gone, but he just could not regain any ambition, hope or motivation. He cherished his unforgiveness and shared it with anyone who would listen. Jack desperately wanted to find closure, but he certainly was not looking in the right places. He looked in bars, tried drugs, and sought direction from people who did not have a clue how to do anything more than drag him further into darkness; he still could not find relief.

At that point, he had compounded his problem to a state of hopelessness by continuing to make bad choices. He tried a new relationship, but it was doomed from the start. Convinced there was no such thing as a good woman, he was not going to give away his beat-up and broken heart, just to have it abused again. Besides, what sane woman would get within ten feet of him while he was in this pitiful condition?

His family grieved with him and feared for his well-being. They saw him slipping away and encouraged him to forgive and move on, but he couldn't. Diane did not deserve to be forgiven. Little did he know that his misery was his own. Diane had long since moved on and was not affected by the fact that he had not forgiven her. For some reason, he thought that in not forgiving her he was punishing her, when all he really did was continue to validate her reason for leaving to begin with. By condemning her, he was really condemning himself. Without forgiving her, he could not clear his vision well enough to see the deadly road he was on. There was no longer any black or white; everything was gray; there were no lines to defend or avoid. Nothing had any meaning and all energy was directed at relieving the pain, but perpetuating the pain is the only thing that was accomplished.

One night, he was standing over the toilet in his rented motel room, watching the water go around in the bowl, and he saw everything he ever hoped for, loved, dreamed about, or counted on, going right down the drain; he was powerless to do anything about it. Jack had given away everything that ever meant anything to him, including his own dignity and self-control.

Where your treasure is, there your heart will be, and Jack treasured his unforgiveness. What he gave his time and energy to is what he ended up with: pain. What he sent out was exactly what he got back: misery. Jack found a lot of company along the road, but he couldn't found closure. The simple but difficult task of forgiving himself and Diane could have had an impact on his life and helped him change direction. However, at that point in the journey, Jack did not have the ability or the desire to do much more than wander around in the town of Guilt, looking for some relief. We haven't seen the last of Jack; we will catch up with him again in a later chapter.

Chapter 6

A Plan That Will Bring Freedom

When our lives are operating at their highest and most efficient level, it is love that motivates our thoughts and actions. Love paves the way to the fulfillment of every righteous rule or law that was ever written. Love has a way of creating love, but its continual rebirth begins and ends with each individual. Forgiveness places the responsibility of perpetuating love for self and others directly on each person by stating that for the most part, it is not the events in life that stop the circulation of love, but how we react to those events.

Other people can hurt us physically or emotionally, and they can violate our rights or our space, but we are the ones who have control over how we deal with their actions. Our reaction is what determines the eventual outcome. We either maintain or relinquish our control by choice. When we are wronged, it is ultimately up to us to decide whether we wish to recognize that wrong and work toward resolution or continue to allow the situation to have a negative impact on our life. Will we acknowledge, engage, and work through the pain, or insist on enlarging it? Will we use the situation as an opportunity to grow and treat ourselves to a little love, or nurture our pain and demand payment? There are tools available to help us bring about resolution, and one of the most basic tools is choice.

By choosing not to forgive someone, we are giving them the power to continue to affect our lives and the freedom to influence our futures. Can you afford to allow someone to occupy that kind of space in your mind? Do we really want to give anyone such freedom, or do we want to regain our own freedom by releasing them? Forgiveness is not automatic, and neither is the freedom that comes at the end of the process. Freedom is a precious gift that is worth fighting and sacrificing for.

The beginning of any change starts with the realization that change is both necessary and possible. We must first be in possession of the belief that forgiveness is worth the investment, and understand the challenges that come with the commitment. Only then can we proceed toward success. Along the way, pride and old thinking are sure to hinder progress. Making a real commitment to working through life's trials and being willing to forgive in all circumstances will, at times, be a burden we do not want to deal with, but surrendering pride and old mindsets will bring fruitful results.

Releasing resentment is rarely a one-time affair. You may decide to forgive and believe you have worked through an issue, just to find it popping up again. That is why it is important to be mindful of the goal and remember the eventual reward while we are in the middle of the struggle to free ourselves from the burdens others place on us.

So, at least in part, we can see that arriving at closure in any given situation requires a number of elements coming together, all of which we have control over. We need to be aware of when there is a problem; we have to believe there is a solution; and then, we have to make the choice to proceed in the right direction. In addition, we need to remain committed and willing to stay the course, knowing it will be difficult at times. In the next few pages, we will watch one woman as she struggles to find closure, and we will see if her beliefs, choices, and commitment were able to lead her to the desired destination.

{ Facing Forgiveness Head-on }

Gail follows the same path everyday on her way to work. It takes about forty-five minutes to get from her home to the office. She spends the time during her drive allowing her mind to wander, from reflecting on the past to pondering the future, while the radio plays in the background. Although the time spent traveling to work is an insignificant part of the day, the routine of it is somehow comforting.

On this day, like any other, Gail gets up early and takes the time to carefully prepare herself for the day. After putting on the right outfit and applying her makeup, she looks in the mirror, decides she is satisfied with her efforts, and heads off to work.

Gail drives toward her place of employment on this particular morning, but never makes it to her destination. Without warning, a driver in the oncoming lane crosses over and hits Gail head-on. Nothing can prepare a person for that type of experience. One second, it is life as usual, the same old routine of going from home to work, and in the blink of an eye, there is no routine! The rest of the world continues to move along at its regular pace, but everything has changed for the people who occupy this one little area.

For one brief moment after the impact, there is complete silence that is instantly replaced by chaos. The impact has left both cars demolished. Battery acid and radiator fluid spill onto the hot engines and create a toxic steam. It looks as though an explosion has gone off; there is glass, metal, and plastic spread out in all directions on the instantly formed debris field.

Gail's eyes are open, but she cannot focus on or comprehend what just happened. Her brain does a quick check of her condition and reports to her that she has sustained injuries to her wrists, chest, and neck. All of her vital signs are good, and there are no internal injuries. She has movement in all of her extremities, and although she doesn't know it yet, she has no life-threatening or disabling injuries. As the mind and body struggle frantically to assess the damage and attempt to restore balance, Gail sits quietly without much conscious thought or emotion.

The driver of the other car is a young mother who has her children in the car: a toddler in the back seat and an infant in the front. The woman is, for the most part, uninjured, but tragically, the same cannot be said for the children. The boy in the back suffers a broken leg, and the poor, innocent infant suffers a spinal cord injury that will leave her paralyzed from the neck down for the rest of her yet-to-be-lived life. It is hard to understand how or why the one individual in this tragic scene who cannot even walk or talk is dealt such a harsh blow.

The ambulances and firemen are quickly at the scene of the accident to extract the people from the twisted automobiles and clean up the mess. News reporters are never far behind a situation like this, and the fact that two beautiful children were so badly hurt will give them something to fill the airtime on the evening news. That night, a glimpse of the wreckage and a clip of Gail being put into an ambulance is seen on TV, along with an interview with the tearful and frantic mother of the injured children. The woman's agony can be felt through the television set. The camera is parked right in front of her face while she weeps uncontrollably.

The reporting of this sad incident stirs the emotions of the community, and their compassion moves them to rally together in assisting the young mother and her children. Several local organizations pledge to help with the medical costs, which are certain to rise beyond belief. The needs of the infant will have to be met in a hospital out of town, so others step up and secure transportation and housing for the grieving mother. The news station also helps set up a trust fund for the children. The hearts of people are moved, so they place a portion of their financial means into the children's future.

No one would want to be in a position similar to that of the young mother. No amount of assistance will be able to quiet her mind when she lies down at night and wrestles with the endless guilt that haunts her. God only knows the pain this woman has to endure and the hardship that lies ahead. Hopefully, her emotional wounds will begin to heal and she can forgive herself, so she will not be forever trapped in guilt by this devastating event. There is no way for her to be available for her children in the best possible way, if her thoughts and actions are driven by guilt.

The story quickly dies away in the press, covered up by the next newsworthy event. At last, all of the parties are left with the reality of the situation after the initial shock and adrenaline wear off.

Meanwhile, Gail's wounds are tended to and begin to heal, but lost somewhere in this story is the fact that she is a victim, also. She has sustained wounds that will take more time to heal than her physical injuries. Gail's story is never reported on or followed up, because it just doesn't make good press. After all, it was her car that was involved in the tragic event that ended in those children being so badly injured; never mind the fact that she was traveling at the posted speed limit in her own lane when the accident occurred. None of these truths are lost on Gail; she is the one having to deal with them. Gail is torn in several directions, because she has a very real sympathy for all the other woman is suffering, and her heart is crushed by the idea of what the children are facing. However, Gail also has her own practical and emotional problems to work through as a result of this accident.

Even her husband does not quite understand the emotional trauma placed upon her by this situation. When he first sees her, he briefly inquires about her physical condition, expresses his shock and grief concerning the children, and then begins to interrogate her with a list of typical and practical questions. He wants to know about time, location, estimated costs of damage, and current insurance status—all of the information men need to know to help them get the big picture. Unfortunately, he neglects to inquire about how she was feeling. Her emotional state should have been at the top of his list, but somehow that got overlooked. That particular mistake is not one he will forget or repeat anytime in the near future. Gail makes sure of that.

There are a number of facts about this story that have not yet been revealed, which should be mentioned for the purpose of drawing a more complete picture of how this event has, and will, impact Gail's life. These details are not given in order to create or magnify a villain in this story. As much as we like to have a villain in every tragic story, there are no villains in this one, only victims.

The woman who drove her car into Gail's world was an uninsured motorist. This further complicates the situation, because Gail's insurance is minimal and certainly will not cover all of her losses. Gail's emotional distress is compounded, because she knows from the police report the children in the car were not properly restrained, and this is probably why their injuries were so severe. None of this changes the reality that part of Gail's healing will have to include forgiving the woman who changed her life in many complex ways that day, but it does make her trip toward closure a little more complicated and more difficult.

Gail has been knocked off balance in every way imaginable: physically, financially, and emotionally. Every aspect of her life has been disrupted and is currently being tested. Gail is a faithful woman who appreciates the importance and value of forgiveness. In her life, she has experienced the joy of being forgiven, as well as the freedom that comes from forgiving others. She is determined to work though this situation in a healthy and productive way.

The shock and disbelief of the event quickly dissolves, and if the truth were told, Gail finds herself heading toward anger, carrying with her some pretty heavy resentment. She resents the fact that this woman, whom she has never met, has created this physical and financial hardship in Gail's life. There will be no fair compensation for Gail; she is left to pay her own medical bills, and she has to make arrangements with her employer to cosign a loan in order to get some suitable transportation. Gail also resents the woman for the hardships she has placed upon her own children by causing the crash and not having the children properly restrained. These feelings may not be popular or politically correct, but they are her true inner feelings at this point in the process. It is an odd mixture of helplessness and frustration that Gail finds herself dealing with.

Gail realizes, after a time, that anger is not where she needs to be, so she decides to make the effort to move on. As she is able to drop her resentments and move through anger on toward sadness, she carries with her a nagging sense of guilt. She can't seem to shake this guilty feeling she has concerning the predicament the injured children are in. She knows their circumstances are not her fault, but the guilt continues to weigh on her. Sometimes she relieves herself of the guilt by going back and picking up her resentment toward the children's mother. It is not an easy time for Gail, but she and her husband encourage and strengthen each other by helping one another stay focused on the goal. It may be slow, but progress is being made.

One day, a couple of months down the road, Gail receives a phone call from a lawyer, who states he is representing the woman who caused the accident, and he is in the process of preparing a law suit against Gail. According to him, it does not matter that the accident is not her fault. He explains that because of the injuries to the children in this case, there is the possibility that bad press could be targeted toward any organization that is seen as a villain in this situation. His plan, basically, is to use the sensitive nature of this case to extort money from her insurance company. He also plans to sue the manufacturer of the infant seat, as well as the large chain retailer who sold it. Never mind the fact the child was not strapped into the seat—the threat of looking bad in the public eye will have everyone settling the issue out of court, despite the facts. According to the lawyer, this whole situation is about image and money, not people.

Now Gail faces a new problem, not to mention some new resentments that will have to be worked through. Gail and her husband are tempted to get their own lawyer, fight back, and get their share of the "corporate pie," but they elect to stay the course, knowing that getting involved in this type of battle will surely hinder their progress and take them off their chosen path.

As time goes by, Gail is reminded every month of the commitment she has made to forgive. Her resolve is tested each time a new medical bill or loan payment comes in the mail. When she feels the sting of those bills, she uses it as an opportunity to check within herself to see where her head and heart are. If she finds she is in a place she does not need to be, she has the skills, resources, and determination to move on to a better place.

Gail has found her way to closure in this situation. She is hopeful that everyone who was affected by this tragedy will find closure and use the lessons learned along the way to benefit themselves and others. Gail made a choice to use forgiveness. She weighed the potential rewards of the endeavor against the known consequences of not forgiving, and the choice was simple, but proved tough to carry out. Knowing it would not be quick or easy, she aided herself and shortened her journey, by staying aware of what her mind was thinking and her heart was feeling at all times,. And by using her commitment to redirect herself, when necessary. Gail faced a difficult task head-on and held to her belief that she could only arrive at her desired destination by first going through forgiveness. Her efforts have been rewarded, and she is now in possession of a peace that can only be found on the other side of forgiveness.

{ There Is No Magic }

We can see from Gail's story that there were a number of steps that led up to her being able to relieve herself of the burdens that are inherent to the type of circumstances she was placed under after the accident.

She could have carried around her resentments and all of the other baggage the accident created for years. Sooner or later, she would have gotten used to the extra weight and would not even notice she had not dealt with the issues. But just because something is not constantly rolling around in our conscious mind does not mean that it is gone and cannot affect our lives.

Gail ended up in closure because she knew the requirements; she was familiar with the path from having traveled it before, and she was prepared for the process. *She used awareness to get her bearing, desire to get started, and willingness to endure.* Nothing she did was magic, although it may seem that way when you look up and find yourself on the other side of forgiveness.

{ Trying On A New Look }

Developing new patterns or mindsets in our lives can be difficult, but it is possible. If we are to expect a new output, there will have to be some new input, because actions are always preceded by thoughts. How much thought do you give to the process of tying your shoes? For most people, it has become an automatic reaction that happens when you put your shoes on, but that was not always the case. Learning to master something we can now do without thinking took some effort in the beginning. So it is with everything that we will ever attempt to learn or grow into. From the guy throwing horseshoes in the park, to the woman playing violin at Carnegie Hall, repetition plays a role in how well we develop and mature at any endeavor.

Practice is also an essential element of forgiveness, and like anything else, it starts inside. Regularly taking an open and honest look at all of the people and situations we encounter is a great place to start. Looking at the actions of others, and then examining our reaction, along with how we feel, will tell us where we are, versus where we want to be. If a person happens to be dealing with a situation in which some time has passed since the incident, he can still find out where he is in relation to that person or event, by sitting quietly and allowing his mind to recall the incident and/or people involved. At that point, a person should look inside and ask himself what he is feeling. This method is an effective way of determining whether one is looking at an unresolved issue, or if the issue is closed. If a person is feeling anything other than peace and quietness, then he may need to address the issue. In the following pages, we will take a look at the different emotions and mindsets we all encounter while dealing with the wide variety of uncomfortable and disheartening circumstances which life puts us through. Our hope is to gain a better understanding about where our minds go and where they get stuck, when it comes to working through hardship.

{ Towns along the road }

The road to Closure is a journey that has many different stops along the way. Some of the places we go are unavoidable and are a natural part of the process. The key is to pass through them, and not take up residence in any of these places or continue to travel from one negative place to another.

One of the common first stops people make is at a little town called Blame Bay. When we are hurt, making an honest assessment of who is at fault and to what degree is a legitimate part of healing, but when this is done, it is time to move on. Unfortunately, the town of Blame Bay is overpopulated, because too many people stay there, rather than pass through. This place is filled with people who spend all day talking about who hurt them; that is all they ever do. Nothing ever gets accomplished at Blame Bay. All of the radios and televisions in that town are stuck on the same station.

Port Pride is another interesting community, where the people claim to have no need to go to Closure and forgiveness is never spoken of. Everyone here is absolutely convinced that they are okay, and any talk about feelings or introspection is strictly prohibited. Most of the people who live in Port Pride work at the factory just outside of town, where they produce self-destruction. Farther along, in Doubt Valley, the people are not really confident in themselves or the value of forgiveness. They wonder if people will be receptive to forgiveness, forgetting that the process is for their own well-being. Less than a mile away is Fearsville, a place where the people hold onto their unforgiveness, hoping it will protect them from getting hurt again. Have you ever been to any of these towns?

Procrastination is another place where you can go at any time, day or night, and find a crowd of people standing on the corner of Nowhere, talking about nothing. Just down the road is Isolation. This is not a bad place to pull into and have a look around, or get some rest from time to time. But the ones who live there full-time are not a happy or healthy group. They have either checked out of life or end up moving into Depression, and Depression is never a good town to travel to, because there is no quick or easy way out.

Anger has already been mentioned more than once. This is a place that nearly everyone frequents at some point. Moving into and through Anger is all part of healing, but we need to be sure not to spend too much time at this place, and we certainly do not want to live here. The next stop after Anger should be Sadness, not Revenge. Sadness is a place where we can lay down our resentments, reflect on the situation, and take time to feel the pain, before moving on towards Acceptance. Some people (especially men) tend to avoid stopping at Sadness; they do not want to slow down long enough to feel the pain, but Sadness is a necessary and important stop on the road to Closure.

One place the mind can take us after being hurt is straight to Revenge. This is not a good place to pull over and park, because the people in this town spend their time plotting and conspiring to do harm. They spin their wheels, fantasizing about the great payback, and talk about how sweet it would be to get even. If you spend any length of time here, you might pick up or create some ideas that could turn into actions, which you will regret, and which really serve no purpose—unless, of course, creating more hardship is the objective. Because hardship is the only thing that ever comes out of Revenge.

Obviously, the real objective is to end up in Closure, but all of these other places are legitimate emotions and mindsets we are likely to encounter, and we have to move through them while working toward our goal. The idea is to not go to some of these places to begin with, and to be sure not to get stuck in others. We all have different character traits; one person may be struggling to get out of Anger, while another person may be more likely to get stuck in Fearsville. Whatever the case, we all share some things in common when it comes to getting stuck in any one of these places.

Pride, laziness, and loss of focus are three of the culprits that stagnate progress toward our goal, not to mention that it is our nature to drift toward any number of the towns we examined. Once we are there, it is surprisingly easy to get comfortable and want to stay. No matter where we are, we will always be able to find others at that place, and they will appreciate our company. Cattle feel most comfortable around other cattle, so if we are insistent on justifying or ignoring our unforgiveness, it will never be hard to find people who understand and agree with our position. The danger is that the longer we stay in any given place, soliciting sympathy or magnifying the pain, the more distorted our perception can become. Some of the most unnecessary and harmful acts are carried out by people who go to Revenge with a distorted perception and stay too long.

The way to get out of any of these places is by first knowing where we are and remaining willing to pursue the peace we desire and deserve. We can find our location by simply asking ourselves how we feel about any given person or situation. We should make a note of how long we have been at that location and remember, in the end, that it is in our best interest to move on.

The term "let go" is often used in reference to forgiving. Sometimes in our lives, we may have been advised by a friend to let go of a particular issue and not let it bother us anymore. But rarely is this advice followed by any instruction on just how to go about accomplishing this task, so let's take a little deeper look at letting go. If someone wanted to let go of an apple in his hand, there are several steps that have to come together before even a task this simple can occur. It would first require a conscious desire, followed by a purposeful thought that would direct a physical action, before the apple could be released. Releasing ourselves from any unwanted burdens works in much the same way. Releasing resentments is often more difficult than letting go of an apple because, for some reason, we have a need to keep bending over and picking the resentments back up.

By using the right combination of the things we have access to and control of, like desire, choice, awareness (which we can learn), and commitment, we can treat ourselves to some new freedoms, by releasing resentments and letting go of any and all extra baggage we may be carrying around.

{ There Are No Hamster Wheels In Closure }

The eventual victory might be subtle and quiet, but it will be powerful. We should enjoy it; it was our choice and it is our reward. When we arrive at our destination, our loads will be light. There will be no more pain and no need to rehash the situation. There will be no villains or victims, no need to chase justice or seek payment. There are no hidden agendas or apologies necessary in Closure. All we will be carrying with us is a peace that surpasses all understanding.

Chapter 7

How Do I Forgive Myself

{ First Things First }

It could be argued that a chapter about forgiving ourselves should have been placed at the front of this book. How can we forgive others if we haven't looked at the idea of forgiving ourselves, and worked through some of our own issues? Everyone knows he cannot give away that which he does not possess. On the other side of the coin, we also know one cannot receive that which he is not willing to give. So how can we forgive ourselves if we have not first become familiar with and are committed to forgiving others? We looked at these two principles earlier, and at first glance, they do appear to contradict each other. If you cannot do one thing without first doing the other, then where do you start? Is this some kind of riddle? Can these principles actually hold up under the pressure of practical application, or are they just some lofty theory that has us talking in circles? Actually, the latter part of the last statement is pretty close to the truth, but we are not talking in circles; we are talking about cycles. No spiritual reality can be in conflict with another, so if both of these principles are true, then they must both be somehow working together, and that is, in fact, exactly what they do.

Through forgiving others, we are not only freed from the burdens that have been placed on us, but we are also opened up in a way that makes us better able to receive grace. At the same time, by forgiving ourselves, we are put into a position where we can give away the grace that now rests within us. Grace creates and promotes more grace; it all works together in a magnificent eternal cycle. Where you get started is not important; the idea is to take the first step and have faith that momentum will begin to build and progress will be made.

For some people, it may be easier to start by concentrating on releasing resentments toward others, working outside of self, establishing some new patterns, and obtaining new tools, before attempting to clean their own house. The opposite could easily be true as well. For some, it may be through the forgiveness of self that they are able to begin embracing and nurturing a newly found grace, before sharing it with others.

The Bible says we are to love our neighbor as we love our self.[8] Few people would argue against the value of pursuing this precept, but fulfilling its objective in the intended manner is not a simple task. Our previous studies have shown that, in truth, we can only love our neighbor to the degree that we love ourselves. Unfortunately, self-condemnation brought on by past mistakes haunts many people, and leaves them in a place where they do not have a functional, balanced, and appropriate love of self. So how can we ever expect to love our neighbor or anyone in a proper manner, if we do not love ourselves? If we are not healthy, our relationships will not be healthy—none of them. In order to be able to give and receive love on the deepest levels and in the best possible way, it is crucial to be free from self-condemnation.

[We Are Already Paying A Price; Why Add To It?]

Naturally, there are consequences to all negative actions, and we will pay for the mistakes we make in life, but if we want to move from mistake to lesson, then we have to forgive ourselves. Permanent self-condemnation should not be part of the price we pay for making mistakes. Others may not be willing to forgive and prefer we be punished until some unpayable toll is collected. Sometimes, it is we who impose the penalty of self-condemnation, generated by shame. But our true responsibility is to acknowledge our wrongs, grieve the harm caused, accept the consequences, and learn from the situation. We also have the right and responsibility to move past all of these legitimate stops and on to closure.

The negative effects of unforgiveness are universal, so it does not matter if it is directed toward someone or toward self; either way, there will be a price to pay. In some cases, we may be aware of the fact that our past actions are causing us discomfort. Feeling guilt or shame is part of being on the road to recovery, but getting stuck in guilt or shame serves no purpose and benefits no one. We are the ones who take ourselves to guilt, but we also need to make sure we know how to get out of guilt. Too often, people buy into the idea that they deserve to be forever imprisoned in guilt. That idea needs to die away! One sure way of getting something to die away is to quit feeding it.

In other situations, we may see that the harm we created in the lives of others (although not yet properly dealt with) does not manifest itself in the form of conscious or nagging guilt. We can deny the need for reconciliation to the point where these issues eventually slip, or are pushed, into a deeper and less accessible part of our conscience. They have not gone away; they just sit there, slowly and quietly poisoning our lives and hindering our progress on every level.

It is imperative that we are able to look at and recognize how and when we begin to accumulate self-condemnation. It is just as important to gain some understanding about why some of us tend to stubbornly insist on not forgiving ourselves. Whether we do it knowingly or unknowingly, we are, in effect, creating and perpetuating our own pain. By observing our present thoughts and feelings in reference to the harm we have done to ourselves and others in the past, we can, hopefully, avoid or break the cycle of feeding the poison of unforgiveness to ourselves and others.

We will address the issue of forgiving ourselves from several angles in the coming pages. starting with taking an indirect view of the forgiveness of self, by looking in on a couple of characters we have already met. The road to Closure has many different twists, turns, and unlikely encounters along the way.

{ Daddy's Little Princess }

When we first met Gail in the last chapter, she had been thrust into some extreme hardships and was able to successfully work through them, gaining some wisdom and useful experience in the process. That was at a point in her life when she truly understood the value of grace, and she already knew the treasures that lay on the other side of forgiveness. But you can believe it was not always that way. In Gail's life, just like the rest of ours, victory did not come without some sacrifice, and you can bet her success was also preceded by many failures. Let's take a few steps backward and follow her path, in an attempt to gather for ourselves some insight into why we struggle so much in relationships. How is it that so much damage is created through sabotage and self-destruction? Hopefully, we can glean something from her story that can assist us in our own endeavor to receive and administer the grace that kills guilt and stops the senseless cycle of self-condemnation.

Gail was born into, and raised by, a family who put her needs before their own. She never wanted for anything and was always well-loved. Gail was her father's little princess. The innocence of childhood always fades quickly into the need for adventure that adolescence brings. It was not long before Gail's mind was filled with the curiosity of a cat, and her heart developed the playful and mischievous nature of an otter. She wanted to do everything her mother told her not to do. Since staying away from boys was on the top of her mother's list, naturally boys were one of the first things she wanted to find out about.

She found out quickly enough what boys were about. In the blink of an eye she was in love with a young man, pregnant with her first child, married, and moving onto the next phase of her life before ever really living the first phase.

Within a dozen years, Gail's husband was beginning to come into his own in the business world, where eventually, he would become quite successful. Gail had a total of three beautiful children and they all settled into the routine of being the perfect American family. PTA meetings, musical rehearsals for the youngest child—there were always things to do. Gail took care of being the mother and her husband took care of being the provider, but neither one of them was taking care of the marriage.

Maybe it was the leftover hormones of an unfulfilled adolescence, due to getting married so young; maybe it was the complacency that can come with material success, or possibly just the temptations common to all people; but either way, the result was that Gail and her husband started drifting in opposite directions. Before long, they were spending more time and energy hurting, rather than helping, each other. No issues were ever resolved or worked through; they were ignored, covered up, or used as weapons. After one hurt the other, the wounded partner would scheme to get revenge for the misdeed, and then carry out the plan. In turn, the other would seek his own revenge.

One day, Gail decided she did not want to play this game any longer, so she packed up and walked out. As she closed the door behind her, she bent over to pick up two suitcases to take with her; one was filled with regret and the other with resentment. She also unknowingly walked away with a heart filled with guilt that was sure to take her to some undesirable places unless or until it was dealt with.

{ Jack Is Back }

The last time we saw Jack, he was standing over a toilet, watching the water flush out of the bowl, reflecting on how that was symbolic of his once purposeful and prosperous life. He remained outwardly functional for the most part, but his ignorance in relation to the needs of anyone other than himself, combined with his arrogant and selfish personality, caught up to him, and he was now in a place of despair. He had always had a pretty high opinion of himself and a low opinion of others, but one broken heart changed all of that; his confidence and self-esteem were gone. With an inquisitive mind and the willingness to try anything once, he sought relief under every rock, but could not find it anywhere. Eventually, his resentment toward his ex-wife turned inward. He blamed himself for his heartbroken condition and became convinced he deserved to be miserable. Certainly he was responsible to a large degree for his situation, but his perception was distorted. He was blanketed and consumed by guilt that ended up manifesting itself in all kinds of ugly ways.

{ An Odd Couple, But A Perfect Pair }

There are no signs outside the town of Guilt. The people either do not know, or do not want to know, that they are presently residing in that town. While in Guilt, most people will go to great lengths to deny, cover-up, mask, or ignore the fact that they are in that particular location. There is no recovery or healing going on for the people stuck in Guilt, but there are a lot of things to do there. People think they are having fun and getting things done, but that is never the case.

Gail and Jack come from two different worlds, but they happened to bump into one another while they were both stuck in Guilt. Gail spent most of her time there trying to have fun. She had done the right thing for the wrong reasons for too many years, and now, she had the freedom to do as she pleased. She was looking for some excitement, something or someone a little closer to "the edge."

Jack happened to wander by, and he seemed to be able to supply what Gail was looking for. We know he was living on the edge, but he was not doing it to have fun; he was trying to kill the pain and hide from the fact that he was stuck in Guilt, too. Jack was looking for some comfort or stability without having to make a commitment, and Gail appeared to be willing to get what she wanted by giving Jack what he wanted; they were a perfect match. Of course, neither of them had any real or conscious agenda, because they had not thought that far ahead.

They both dealt with their guilt in different ways, and they each had different motives for wanting to be with the other. Together, they made a bit of an odd couple, but a perfect pair in a sad and unhealthy sort of way. All one could really offer the other was a temporary distraction from the fact that neither one of them was happy or complete. The relationship had disaster written all over it from the start, but they thought it was a great deal, because each one could get their shallow needs met without having to give too much in return.

Gail's friends were not impressed with her selection of playmates, and Jack's family wondered about Gail's motives. The two of them did not care, because what each one represented to the other was an escape from reality. Neither one of them was really doing anything for themselves or for the relationship, but somehow, the unlikely connection was held together by what little bit of themselves they were giving. After some time, they actually started to grow on each other, and a deeper bond began to form.

The fact that they were bonding interested Gail, but it scared Jack. He wanted desperately to love someone and to be loved, but he dared not go down that road again. Besides, he was having too much fun being miserable; why change a good thing? Gail knew Jack had some issues, but her nesting and nurturing instincts kicked in, and she focused on Jack's potential, not his baggage. She looked at him like a project. She would fix him up and then he would be a keeper.

No one knows how people get to a point where they secretly believe they deserve to be miserable, but that is where Jack ended up. Even though he loved Gail, he could not give himself to the relationship. He had too many unresolved issues from his last broken heart. He was suspicious of anyone who wanted to love him, because, in his twisted thinking, he was not lovable. He had destroyed his marriage, hurt his children, and wrecked his career, so why on earth would Gail want anything to do with him? The result of his backward thinking took Jack further down the road of self-destruction.

Gail was up for living on the edge for a while, but that got old, and she wanted something different. She certainly did not want to go up to and over the edge, so she had to step back as Jack's multi-level misery lead him up to and over some lines Gail was not willing to cross. Jack continued to run from reality, unwilling and unable to work toward resolution in any area of his life. When you mix misery and desperation, what you have is a formula for disaster, and that was a picture of Jack—a walking disaster that eventually led to prison.

His family was quietly relieved, because they were concerned for his safety, and they knew his state of mind. Gail's friends and family were equally relieved, but for different reasons. Now Gail could be rid of Jack and move on with her life. Gail was frustrated; she thought she could fix Jack. Now her project and her distraction were gone, and all she had really managed to do was accumulate more baggage to add to that which she was already carrying around. Now at least she could have a clean break from Jack, or so she thought.

Jack was sent away to pay his debt to society and live out the consequences of his actions, and Gail prepared to regroup and move on with her life. This would appear to be the end of another sad story about two people hurting themselves by staying stuck in guilt. However, we already know from our original encounter with Gail in the last chapter that she is destined for better places.

For some reason, even though Jack and Gail knew their once sickly relationship was now dead, neither one of them could quite let go altogether. It was at that time, during separate and almost simultaneous events, that God placed a seed of faith and a portion of grace in the hearts of Gail and Jack. God has been in the business of saving souls and changing hearts since the beginning of time. Real hope and new direction can be found in the Lord, even in the darkest of situations.

While sitting in the local county jail, Jack was visited by a man who led him onto the path of new hope and eternal life through Jesus Christ. Gail's life reached a turning point during the same week. While attending a morning service at her sister's church, she felt drawn to the altar at the end of the service. Gail surrendered her burdens and baggage to God, and walked away with a quiet sense of peace and comfort. This new peace that she was now in possession of would prove to be strong enough to sustain her, despite the many trials on the road ahead.

The good news was that their old relationship was dead, thanks to Jack. There was really no aspect of their old connection that was worth saving, anyway. The whole time that they were a couple, the only thing that bonded them together was guilt and selfishness. Each put their own desires first, and those desires were motivated by a need to ignore or cover up the underlying guilt they both had from mistakes in the past, for which they had never forgiven themselves.

The odds of their relationship being able to work and to grow in a healthy direction would have been bad under normal conditions, but the fact that they planned to attempt this while Jack was still incarcerated made the success of this undertaking all but impossible. If they had any chance at all, old things would have to pass away, and all things would have to become new.

{ A New Beginning }

They were not ready to deal with their own personal guilt, so they began this journey by first learning to embrace God's forgiveness, then looking at the resentments they had for one another. Realizing the abuse in their relationship had worked both ways made releasing these particular resentments a good place to start. Taking an honest look at their own actions, and understanding that they had played a significant role in perpetuating the dysfunction of the relationship brought them up to and over their first hurdle. They each made this fundamental first step, working together through open communication. That was the beginning of an entirely new life for them as individuals and as a couple.

The only way to build trust is by first being vulnerable. So by becoming willing to open up and expose their pain and guilt to each other, a very real healing was able to take place, and the relationship between them started to bear fruit. They were able to give and receive love on new and exciting levels.

As they came to a point where they each valued the needs of the other more than their own, this reborn relationship was no longer made up of two different people, because the two had become one. They made a covenant to put the needs of their new marriage above their own, and they vowed always to work through any and all difficulties with a willingness to forgive one another, regardless of the seriousness of the infraction.

This vow to forgive in all circumstances may have looked like a license to do whatever one pleased, knowing he, or she, would be forgiven. In some respects, it was a license—a license to do what their hearts wanted, which was to honor the marriage. This vow actually worked to strengthen the bond between them. They now knew from personal experience that the process of openly and honestly addressing issues between them, when one had hurt the other, was a tough and discomforting undertaking for both parties. They did not want to create that type of work for themselves. Running from, denying, and covering up their actions was no longer an option, so they were motivated to quickly resolve any issues that came up. Ironically, they discovered purely by accident that putting the needs of the marriage first was actually the best way to have their own needs met.

Jack and Gail cherish each other, treasure their time together, and remain grateful for the experience of being able to travel on the road to closure as true and healthy partners. The place their journey has taken them has left them with a deep appreciation for life. Having been to some very dark places, they are truly grateful for the light and the love in which they now live. Their relationship is grounded in grace, rather than guilt. There have certainly been some growing pains along the way, and their vows have been tested, also, but with each failure, their love is strengthened. They cannot change their past or fix some of the damage they caused, but they have both cleaned up their own wreckage and forgiven themselves. They have benefited from their past and now use it to help create a better future. They are still a bit of an odd couple, but they truly are a perfect pair.

The story of Jack and Gail gives us an accurate picture of the potential cost of creating our own hardship and then holding onto it. Their story also shows us the possible rewards for taking the steps to allow our pasts to be what they are, without controlling or having a negative impact on our futures. By watching Jack and Gail's life unfold, we were able to observe how these two people accumulated their guilt, how it affected them, why they held onto it, and what it took to finally let it go.

As we move on to look at the hows and whys of forgiving ourselves, it would be good to examine these points from a personal perspective. Let us search within ourselves as this chapter winds down, to see how this subject relates to us individually, because we will not know if we are at the point of closure on any given issue, unless we first check inside to see where we are. Another way to ascertain our present location is to look around outside of ourselves. The people we spend time with and the places toward which we gravitate is an indication of what is currently driving our lives and where we are. Anyone who takes the time to look inside and/or outside himself in an attempt to discover where he is has already made it at least halfway toward his desired destination.

{ Judge Not, Lest You Be Judged }

It is easy to be tough on people when they make mistakes. Something about judging others seems to appeal to our nature. However, we need to be careful in this area, because judgment is a two-way street. Ironically, we are often the ones who fulfill the reality of the spiritual principle, which relates to being judged in the manner by which we judge others. When we make mistakes, the same harsh judgment we use against other people may actually be turned inward. We can effectively give ourselves a dose of our own poison and begin heading in the direction of self-condemnation. This particular scenario is a somewhat unusual example of getting back exactly what we send out. Since self-condemnation is not a healthy or productive place, it is a wise person who examines and monitors the manner by which he or she makes judgments.

There are some twisted advantages of being caught up in self-condemnation that may quietly lure us to that place. There are no expectations of a victim, even if we are our own victims. Resting alone in our misery takes us out of the game of life, so we do not have to set legitimate goals and put forth the effort we really should. That might sound like an unreasonable or unrealistic scenario, but it happens; we just saw it demonstrated in Jack's life.

There is another common occurrence that leads to self-condemnation that should be discussed here. When we hurt someone, especially someone we care about, their decision about whether to forgive us or not should not be the determining factor of whether we proceed with the process of forgiving ourselves. If they wish to continue to hold on to resentments, it is their choice, but it is a dangerous thing to allow their thoughts or decisions to influence our well being. We must forgive ourselves, regardless of what other people do. You are in no way honoring yourself, your faith, or the people you hurt, by handing down the penalty of self-condemnation. Even when others judge us as unworthy of forgiveness, it is in our best interest to acknowledge the wrong, deal with the outcome of our actions, and forgive ourselves. The load life places on us is heavy enough, so there is no reason to increase the load by refusing to release ourselves from the potentially paralyzing burdens of past mistakes.

{ Why Bother? }

Forgiving yourself does not mean that you are not sorry for your actions. Remorse is normal, and a good sign that a person genuinely regrets his actions and is aware of the damage caused, but magnifying remorse is unreasonable and unhealthy.

No one else can do this except us. Only we can forgive ourselves, and that is why we need to bother with this process. If left undone, who suffers? Forgiving ourselves is a win-win deal; we do the giving and receiving. It does not get any better than that. Unfortunately, many people do not believe they deserve this gift. Remember, we teach others how to treat us by the way we treat ourselves.

{ So What If I Don't Bother? }

Negative thoughts are alive in the sense that they can have an effect in the physical world. They can affect our bodies, as discussed earlier, and they can be manifested in the world through our actions. That is why holding onto unforgiveness is so harmful. Pent-up guilt leaves us unable or unwilling to trust, and healthy relationships must be rooted in trust. If we do not trust ourselves, then naturally, we do not trust others, and that puts us in a position where we either cannot make a commitment or we continue to make the wrong commitments. If the perception of ourselves is distorted because of unforgiveness, how can we expect to view and value others in a proper manner?

{ There Is Always Something In The Way }

There are a number of influences that can hinder our progress as we try to regain balance and move in the right direction. The people we have hurt may not want us to heal. Society in general can be unforgiving, and even the people who try to help (the people on our side) can slow or stop progress. Well-meaning people can actually compound the problem of trying to forgive ourselves by minimizing the situation or acting as if this difficult ordeal is simple. Have you ever had someone say, "All you need to do is let that go and move on? God has forgiven you, so why are you not forgiving yourself?" Loved ones can unknowingly chastise and condemn us, even though their motives are to help. Their statements and encouragement may be true and honest, but you cannot just blink your eyes and have everything instantly become better. At least, that is not how it works for most people. It is a process, and we need to not only remember that for ourselves, but we need to be sensitive to this fact when others we know and care about are struggling with forgiveness.

The largest roadblock we will ever face can be found by taking a look in the mirror. Ultimately, we are the ones who feed the destructive cycles associated with poor self-worth, and it is our thoughts and actions that can bring us back into proper balance. We need to play an active role in our own emotional health.

{ Use The Tools }

We have the necessary skills at our disposal to bring about change. One concept we have not looked at is the idea that sometimes we just have to sit still and let the old tapes play—not trying to shut them off, but letting them run their course; understanding that past events will not change, but that we can. In time, the pain and humiliation associated with those tapes will fade, because we have accepted them for what they are, learned from the mistakes, and moved on. Acceptance of self is big news, and it brings with it a healthy perception, the right direction, and new freedom.

CONCLUSION

{In Memory Of Jake}

When the old man named Jake died, back in the first chapter of this book, it was pointed out that he passed away in a state of mind and in a place he had spent a lot of time: Anger.

It may be a bit of a surprise, but a memorial service was held for the lonely old man, and a number of people attended. Actually, when you consider where Jake died and think about the type of people he spent his time around, it becomes clear that the memorial was probably organized more for the people who attended than for the guest of honor. The people who live in the places where he roamed are always hungry for a distraction, and are quick to huddle around and observe the final outcome of self-destruction.

There was quite a variety of people in attendance—most of them from the negative end of the character spectrum. The hypocrites came, acting as if their lives were in order and looking disappointed about the passing of Jake. The slighters were also there, grouped together and lying to one another about the quality of their own lives, while totally denying the fact that Jake was a miserable man. There were those who stood in a place of indifference, ignoring the dysfunction of their own lives, and of Jake's, as well.

No one seemed willing to look at the sad reality of the situation. If they did, they might have to admit the part they played, either directly or indirectly, toward assisting Jake in his self-destruction. Naturally, the busy bodies showed up. They never miss an opportunity to gather around some unfortunate situation and gossip about everyone in attendance. Their heart rates quicken and their adrenaline flows as they sharpen and throw their spears into the back of anyone not watching.

The scoffers and the blamers stood around, stirring up and sharing their general discontent with each other. It was business as usual; everyone was quite satisfied and comfortable in his or her misery. The focus was never really on the life or loss of Jake. The hypocrites were the ones who put the memorial service together. They had programs printed up with their names on them, so everyone would know they had done the right thing. Some of them got up and read scripture, or had some appropriate remarks to share. They would certainly never want to appear as though they did not care.

If that story seems a bit cynical or even dark, consider this thought: there is a part of us which knows and understands every person who showed up at Jake's memorial. A piece of each of those people lives within us to one degree or another. Granted, they were all from the negative end of the spectrum, but that is where Jake spent all of his time. The point of the story is to give a brief but realistic glimpse of some of the less than desirable aspects that are a part of our character.

There is one way of protecting ourselves from getting caught up and becoming dominated by negative thoughts that can lead us to places in which we cannot afford to spend much time. It is by understanding that the potential for these unhealthy character traits truly exists. Bad company corrupts good character, so if we spend too much time in negative places, we are, in effect, feeding those traits, and without a doubt, they will begin to grow.

We will meet many different people along the road. Every one of those people is valuable, and each encounter has the potential to become a useful and treasured experience. Good or bad, we will see a part of ourselves in everyone we meet. If we look, listen, and learn, we will be able to see which part of ourselves needs to be fed and nurtured and encouraged to grow; we will also see which part needs to be neglected and left to die away.

Jake fed the monster and the monster ate Jake. His is a sad story, but one that we should still appreciate and from which we can learn. He got to the point where he could not value anything or anyone, because he did not value himself. Jake got caught by the Golden Rule. Everyone knows the Golden Rule; we should treat others the way we wish to be treated.[9] Not unlike the other spiritual principles we have looked at, the golden rule has more to it than can be seen at the surface. It is much more than some old moral law we should aspire to follow in order to be good people. It is as much a warning as it is a command, because the truth is that you will treat others the way you treat yourself. In the long run, you will be treated the way you treat others. These truths will never change or go away. If we do not value ourselves and treat ourselves well, how can we expect to treat others correctly? On the other side, if we do not value and treat others correctly, what does that say about how much we value ourselves? The spiritual principles examined in this book all run along parallel lines. They can and should assist us in growing and maturing as people, but their value to us as individuals is limited by the degree to which we recognize and appreciate their truth.

Jake's story is a true one, like the story of every person whose life we looked into and followed. These are real people, and all of them, with the exception of Jake, bounced back from some tough situations to live complete and balanced lives. They used forgiveness to take back control of the direction of their lives. They saved themselves future grief and avoided many pitfalls by remembering the lessons learned and using the skills picked up along the way. Awareness and commitment were a key to their successes. In situations where loved ones were involved, it was also the releasing of pride and unreasonable expectations, followed by open communication, which led to eventual freedom.

Hopefully, the stories of the people we have looked at have had a positive impact and can serve as encouragement. Helping us to remember and have confident faith in the fact that no matter where the pain and discomfort comes from in life—whether from places outside our control, from a loved one, or from the person you see in the mirror each day—there are safe, effective, and healthy ways of seeking and finding peace.

The object of this journey has been to help bring us into a greater awareness of ourselves, and to examine the patterns we have developed regarding accumulating and releasing resentment, pain, and burdens. We hope to walk away from this experience with some new knowledge about ourselves, having also identified some of the paths we typically, or automatically, go down when it comes to forgiveness. All things combined, it is sincerely hoped that for many, some new and more prosperous paths have been located for future exploration while on this journey.

Some of the toughest situations you will ever go through can end up bringing about a greater good in your life. So when you feel hurt, beat up, or knocked off course, expect to spend some time in disbelief and be angry about the injustice of it all. Allow the sadness to soak in; feel the pain before you move past that place. Then, you can come into acceptance, with your sights on forgiveness. On the other side of forgiveness, you will find closure. Be certain to remember where you are, how you got there, and how good it feels, because you will surely have to find your way back again in the future. Every time you arrive, share your experience with others and invite them to join you, because you will be in a position to assist them on the road to closure.

END NOTES

1. Dr. Douglas K. Smith, "Who's to Blame", Psychology and You, *Santa Ynez Valley Times*

2. <u>Acts 20:35b</u> Remembering the words the Lord Jesus himself said: 'It is more blessed to give than to receive.' *New International Version (NIV)*

3. W.E. Vine, *Vines Expository Dictionary* (Nashville, Tennessee, Thomas Nelson Publishers, 1985) 86, 250

4. Trent C. Butler, *Holman's Bible Dictionary* (Nashville, Tennessee, Holman Bible Publishers, 1991) 510

5. <u>Exodus 21:23-25</u> But if there is serious injury, you are to take life for life, eye for eye, tooth for tooth, hand for hand, foot for foot, burn for burn, wound for wound, bruise for bruise. New International Version (NIV)
   <u>Leviticus 24:19-20</u> If anyone injures his neighbor, whatever he has done must be done to him: fracture for fracture, eye for eye, tooth for tooth. As he has injured the other, so he is to be injured. *New International Version (NIV)*

6. <u>Matthew 6:14-15</u> For if you forgive men when they sin against you, your heavenly Father will also forgive you. But if you do not

forgive men their sins, your Father will not forgive your sins. *New International Version (NIV)*

7. <u>Matt. 7:12</u> So in everything, do to others what you would have them do to you, for this sums up the Law and the Prophets._*New International Version (NIV)*

   <u>Luke 6:37</u> Do not judge, and you will not be judged. Do not condemn, and you will not be condemned, Forgive, and you will be forgiven. *New International Version (NIV)*

8. <u>Mark 12:29-31</u> "The most important one," answered Jesus, "Is this: 'Hear, O Israel, the Lord our God, the Lord in one. Love the Lord your God with all your heart and with all your soul and with all your mind and with all your strength.' The second is this: 'Love your neighbor as yourself.' There is no commandment greater than these. *New International Version (NIV)*

   <u>Romans 13:9-10</u> The commandments, "Do not commit adultery," "Do not murder," "Do not steal," "Do not covet," and whatever other commandment there may be, are summed up in this one rule: "Love your neighbor as yourself." Love does no harm to its neighbor. Therefore love is the fulfillment of the law. *New International Version (NIV)*

9. <u>Matt. 7:12</u> So in everything, do to others what you would have them do to you, for this sums up the Law and the Prophets. *New International Version (NIV)*

COMMENTS OR QUESTIONS CAN BE ADDRESSED TO

ROADTOCLOSURE@EARTHLINK.NET.

WE WOULD LOVE TO HEAR FROM YOU.

www.ingramcontent.com/pod-product-compliance
Lightning Source LLC
Chambersburg PA
CBHW031233280526
45784CB00004B/1563